MW01531382

MARKING MILESTONES AND MAKING MEMORIES FOR YOUTH

LOOKING BACK . . . LOOKING FORWARD

Copyright © 2004 by Abingdon Press. All rights reserved.

With the exception of those items so noted, no part of this work may be reproduced or transmitted in any form or by any means, electronic or mechanical, including photocopying and recording, or by any information storage or retrieval system, except as may be expressly permitted by the 1976 Copyright Act or in writing from the publisher. Requests for permission should be addressed to Abingdon Press, 201 Eighth Avenue, South, P.O. Box 801, Nashville, TN 37202-0801.

All Scripture quotations, unless otherwise noted, are taken from the *New Revised Standard Version of the Bible,* copyright © 1989, Division of Christian Education of the National Council of the Churches of Christ in the United States of America. Used by permission. All rights reserved.

Scripture quotations marked (NIV) are taken from the HOLY BIBLE, NEW INTERNATIONAL VERSION®. NIV®. Copyright © 1973, 1978, 1984 by International Bible Society. Used by permission of Zondervan Publishing House. All rights reserved.

04 05 06 07 08 09 10 11 12 13—10 9 8 7 6 5 4 3 2 1

MANUFACTURED IN THE UNITED STATES OF AMERICA

Cover and interior design by Keely Moore

A big thank you to **David Stewart** for the thumbprints poster (page 51), the calendar layout ideas (pages 104–105), the witness statement handout (page 106), and the senior banquet and recognition designs (pages 108–109).

At the time of publication, all website addresses were correct and operational.

MARKING MILESTONES AND MAKING MEMORIES FOR YOUTH

LOOKING BACK . . . LOOKING FORWARD

BY JASON SCHULTZ

ABOUT THE WRITER

Originally from Mesa, Arizona, Jason Schultz began his ministry in 1990 as a huddle coach with Fellowship of Christian Athletes and started working with The United Methodist Church in 1992. During his twelve years as a youth minister, Jason has served churches in Virginia, Tennessee, and Washington.

Jason is Director of Youth Ministries at Edmonds United Methodist Church in Edmonds, Washington, just north of Seattle, where he lives with his wife, Laura. He has a Bachelor of Arts degree from the University of Washington, Tacoma, where he studied arts, media, and culture.

CONTENTS

Introduction...........................7

Chapter 1: Games, Retreats, and Events...9

Chapter 2: Family, Gender-Specific, and
Intergenerational Activities....29

Chapter 3: Identity Markers 39

Chapter 4: Tearjerkers 53

Chapter 5: Service and Outreach 63

Chapter 6: Holidays and
Annual Occasions................75

Chapter 7: Milestones 87

Chapter 8: Fundraisers 95

Dedication

This book is dedicated first and foremost to God. I thank God for giving me the gifts for youth ministry and for the many blessings that come from being in ministry with youth.

Secondly, this book is dedicated to my wife, Laura, who has sacrificed countless hours, days, and weeks of "normal" existence so that we can live God's calling. Her love of God, along with lots of patience, support, and understanding makes her the perfect partner. For helping at youth events and for living with all of the late-night calls, weekends away, and toilet paper in our trees, I thank you, Beautiful!

—Jason B. Schultz

INTRODUCTION

During my years of youth ministry, I have compiled many memories, but one stands out as truly special. At a Youth Specialties sabbath retreat in Nashville, Tennessee, I met Mike Yaconelli, the founder of Youth Specialties. I had always wanted to meet this youth leader, whom I considered a hero. One evening during the retreat, I was enjoying a late supper with some fellow youth workers when Mike came over to talk to us. During our conversation, Mike said something that stuck with me: There are few, if any, original ideas in youth ministry, and most ideas are reused. As we often do with heroes, I had built Mike up to be a super guru, assuming he was creative enough to come up with all of the great ideas I had been using for years. But instead of being an egomaniac who claims credit for those thoughts, Mike said even he used other people's ideas in his ministry.

When I heard Mike discuss using and passing on ideas so that other youth leaders could be better equipped in their ministries, I had an epiphany: God's call to reach and empower youth to live for Christ and change the world is bigger than any one person. It is a shared calling, and youth workers should discuss their ideas and experiences so that all of our ministries will be as successful as God wants them to be.

It is with that purpose, and in the vein of Mike's message, that MARKING MILESTONES AND MAKING MEMORIES FOR YOUTH is written. This book contains ideas, stories, and experiences of youth workers around the world. Where applicable (and where I remember), I give credit for my own thoughts, but most ideas in this book have simply been passed on from youth worker to youth worker. These ideas will help your teens grow closer to one another and closer to God. Whether your group is just starting or well established, you will find ideas that make lasting memories in the lives of youth.

This book is not a guide for weekly lessons, because these activities, projects, and milestones extend beyond everyday happenings. Some ideas fit one-time events, and others can be used on an ongoing basis. Pick ideas to enhance your program, retreat, camp, and overall ministry. But please don't try to implement every idea in this book at once—you won't have enough energy!

Use this book as a resource for enhancing your ministry and touching kids' lives in new ways. Some ideas will be new to you, some you may have already done, and some you'll recognize as variations of old favorites. Choose what works best in your ministry.

Create a spiritual scrapbook for your group as you look back and remember the life-changing, soul-shaping moments and look forward to a life of meaningful memories.

God bless,

Jason Schultz

CHAPTER 1
GAMES, RETREATS, AND EVENTS

Games, retreats, and special events are great ways to create memories that last.

Youth love to play games, and most teens like competition. But sometimes competition gets the best of us and our focus shifts from accomplishing a task to winning at any cost. Often people's feelings get hurt. Instead of pitting youth against one another, the games in this chapter challenge them to work together as a group. These games unite the group in competing against time or themselves as a whole rather than divide the youth.

Just as certain games help teens focus on a positive goal, so can retreats. Given this name because they involve retreating from our everyday routine and surroundings, retreats have been practiced for thousands of years. Even Jesus retreated into the wilderness following his baptism to focus

and prepare himself for ministry. When we need re-energizing, we retreat to places of rest and solitude. These getaways can be used to help teens focus, to allow them to grow closer as a group, or to just have fun. Whatever your reason, this chapter provides retreat ideas that are sure to touch youth and leave lasting memories.

When you plan youth gatherings, do you look for activities that are more meaningful than bowling, miniature golf, and game night? If so, this chapter will provide assistance. These events require more than driving to the nearest bowling alley but will be worth the effort because the youth will remember them long after they've forgotten the score of fifty-eight they bowled.

GAMES

ROPES-AND-CHALLENGE COURSE

A ropes course provides one of the best activities for building self-esteem and community in your group. These carefully designed challenges will help your teens grow closer while having lots of fun. A ropes course brings out youths' zeal for competition but makes them focus it on beating the challenge instead of beating one another.

You will find two main types of ropes courses: upper and lower. Upper elements offer challenges that take place above the ground, often twenty to forty feet in the air. Lower elements have challenges on ground level. Typically, upper ropes courses focus on strengthening individuals, while lower ropes courses focus on teamwork and the value of each person in the group.

One reason ropes courses are so successful is that youth see these challenges as "games" and get caught up in the challenge of overcoming seemingly difficult circumstances. While having fun, they learn to trust one another, include every group member in a particular activity, think creatively, solve problems (without help from adult leaders), and develop leadership skills. All of these aspects will help your youth grow closer.

You can easily recreate some lower elements at your local church, but for the full experience contact a local camp or retreat center with a ropes or challenge course. Places that offer ropes courses also have licensed guides to lead your group safely through a meaningful, challenging, and growing experience.

Because ropes courses are an intense bonding experience, this activity works well as an exercise for a small group, such as a Bible study group, leadership team, or confirmation class.

For more ideas on cooperation games and other fun activities, check out the CDs *Team Building & Group Development to Inspire Youth* (ISBN 0-87-014-4) and *Ice Breakers & Openers to Inspire Youth Groups* (ISBN 0-87-34059-4; Abingdon Press, 2004).

TOUR DE (YOUR CITY OR CHURCH NAME HERE)

Many times, games divide your group and pit the youth against one another, resulting in winners and losers. If you prefer games that challenge your youth to work together to beat the clock, competing against time rather than one another, read on.

This game will require you to develop a scavenger hunt, obstacle course, or challenge quest that takes the youth on a tour of your town. Set a time limit by which the group must return with all or as many as possible of their objectives accomplished. Use a kitchen timer with a ringing bell or buzzer. A loud ticking sound at the beginning adds to the excitement of the game as the group heads out. A little music, such as "Theme from Mission: Impossible" (*Mission: Impossible—Music From and Inspired by the Motion Picture*) also makes the game fun.

Just as the Tour de France leads cyclists on a journey through different parts of France, make sure your tour leads the kids through different parts of your town. Send the clues along with a volunteer who gives them to the group after verifying that it has met the requirements at each stop. For fun, take a video camera along and tape the goofiness; teens love to watch themselves later!

The objectives at each stop in the tour can be serious, humorous, or a mixture of both. Feel free to come up with ideas or use the following to get started:

- The entire group has to do headstands in front of a local landmark.

- Get ten strangers to autograph someone's forehead.

- Sing "Up on the Housetop" in a grocery store.

- As cars drive by, get five to honk at the group.

- Recruit two strangers to play a game of leapfrog with the group.

To add a twist, have a volunteer at each stop holding an index card of a Bible verse and making sure someone in the group memorizes the verse before the group advances to the next stage. Each teen may be used for only one stop. At the end of the game, everyone in the group should have memorized at least one verse. Require the entire group to recite the verses—in the order they appear in the Bible—before the timer sounds.

Another unique variation to this game is to designate church members' houses as stops and ask the group to find out something about each person whose house they visited.

WALK-A-MILE

One of the great episodes of the old TV show *The Twilight Zone* was called "A Quality of Mercy," which was featured in the motion picture. The episode deals with a man who is extremely intolerant of another group of people. One day, after his ire peaks, the man steps out of his life and into the life of one of the people he hates. By the end of the episode, the man has "walked in the shoes" of the group he attacked at the beginning of the episode. The man realizes that his treatment of others was wrong and has a new appreciation for that group of people and their differences.

Invite your group to walk in someone else's shoes for an experience they'll remember.

Step 1. Have your students think of an experience that would be completely different from their normal life. For instance, if you have some wealthy kids, they might become poor for the week, wearing only thrift-store clothes and eating meager meals. Some of your youth may take for granted their physical abilities, so they could be blind, deaf, or in a wheelchair for the day. Your girls could even appear as pregnant teens for a day.

You want your students to stop taking for granted what they have and develop empathy for those who live with less than they do or face difficult situations.

Step 2. Decide when the walk-a-mile will take place, and have each youth decide how he or she will become "different." The teens may mimic the behavior of their character and strive for an authentic appearance using costumes, makeup, bodysuits, and so forth.

Step 3. Following their "day (or week) in the life," ask the teens the following questions:

- How did you feel?
- Was the walk easy or difficult? Why?
- How did people treat you? Was that treatment different from how the group you're representing is treated?
- Did you feel judged?
- Did anyone make fun of you? If so, did you see yourself in any of them?
- How will you look at, approach, and treat people in this group now?
- How does God see people who are "different"?
- What are you taking away from this experience?
- How has it changed your life?

WORLD DINNER

Use this game to expose students to the reality that many people face on a daily basis: the lack of basic needs, such as food and water. Publicize the event as a world dinner with food from countries all around the globe. The youth will expect Mexican, Chinese, Italian, or Indian cuisine. In reality, your youth will experience the hardship of hunger and thirst that people in many countries deal with.

Before the dinner, get a list of world populations by consulting an atlas or by going to www.infoplease.com and typing population of countries into the search field. Decide which countries will be represented, and have some statistics about population, hunger, socioeconomic status, and major industries.

Step 1. As your students arrive for dinner, divide them into groups by country. Make the groups' sizes representative of their countries' populations. (For example, the China group would have many more teens than the Iceland group.) When you've divided the groups, have each one sit at the table displaying its country's name. Some countries may have many people, and other countries may have only one person. You can represent a small country with half a person by having one person walk on his or her knees and sit at a TV tray instead of a table.

Since the United States is the center of the universe for some kids, place the US table in the middle of the room with other countries surrounding it. If possible, place geographically distant countries further away from the US, and countries such as Mexico and Cuba nearby.

Step 2. Now it's time for dinner. Start by serving the United States with a lavish, plentiful meal, which should include food teens are used to eating. (If you can't arrange a home-cooked meal, bring in food from your group's favorite local fast-food restaurant.) Bring out the meal so that everyone can see it, walking by other countries before placing it on the US table. Make sure the table is filled with lots of plates, utensils, and napkins, as well as a decorative centerpiece. For drinks, serve clean water (bottled water works) and cans of soda.

Since you want the youth to grasp is that the US (and maybe even the youth group) wastes a lot of food, provide enough food so that the US table will have leftovers. Normally, I don't encourage games that waste food, since so much need exists in the world, but the leftovers can help teach youth the value of food. Make use of any leftovers, either for future meetings or for delivery to a community kitchen.

Step 3. Now serve the other countries. Groups will be expecting the same grand treatment but with food from their countries. Instead, serve the other countries bowls of rice, dry lettuce, and stale bread—again, proportionally by country. Some countries may receive all three, some just one or two, and some will receive nothing. The serving sizes should represent a country's socioeconomic and agricultural condition. Some countries might receive only one bowl of rice for everyone to share, while another country might have a bowl for each person.

For drinks, serve tap water at room temperature. For countries that don't have clean drinking water, add chocolate syrup to each glass to simulate the unfiltered, untreated water the people in those countries drink. Use clear glasses that allow students to see the amount and clarity of the water they receive. Some glasses should be full, and others should have just a teaspoon.

Step 4. By this point, you will wish you had earplugs. If your youth are normal, they will complain about the meal they've received. If you thought they whined before, just wait until they have hard bread and dirty water sitting in front of them while their friends are eating a delicious meal. Don't panic—this pouting is what you want to happen. As the youth complain, resist the temptation to ease their pain, telling them there is nothing you can do about the situation. Let the game unfold and monitor the different groups' reactions to their meals. Some youth may try to take food from the tables that have more, some may like the rice, and some may refuse to eat. Someone may also mix as many different food items into one glass then dare others to drink the mixture. Do not interfere with the

actions and reactions of the youth unless they get too physically or vocally mean. Use their behavior as an illustration during the discussion that follows the meal.

After the US group is done eating and the protests are over, have the youth take their original seats. Ask the youth if they enjoyed their meal, and let them respond. Make sure to point out the leftovers at the US table.

Step 5. Lead the group in a discussion of what happened during meal time. Ask:

- What did you and your countries receive? Was it enough for everyone?
- Are you full? still hungry? satisfied?
- What did you think of the United States' meal? Why was it fair or unfair? How does this meal represent reality?
- How can we be better stewards of our resources?
- What efforts can we make to provide for persons who struggle with hunger?

WORLD DINNER EXPANSION

Give each country transportation, technology, money, food, and military cards made from paper of different colors. Distribute the cards to the countries proportionally, according to their socioeconomic status. Some countries may have more of one item, while another country lacks an item altogether. (For instance, the US would have more technology cards than Laos.) The more cards a country possesses in a category, the stronger that category.

Each group then elects one person to represent its country in worldwide negotiations, where countries can meet one on one (like the United Nations). Treaties can be established, trade agreements made, allies aligned, and so forth. Each country works to get what it lacks by going to other countries. The only catch is that a country must possess a card of a category to use that category. For instance, you must have a transportation card to travel to another country, and a military card to defend yourself.

As facilitator, randomly throw natural disasters at a country. You may knock out a country's food, technology, military, or transportation for a while, during which it surrenders its cards to you. For pollution violations, take away technology cards. When a country's pollution has ruined a neighboring country's crops, take away one of the victim's food cards. You can also create an invasion, oil blockade, hostage situation, and so on, by a simple declaration; countries will then decide what to do. Students will soon learn their actions have ramifications on other countries because of treaties and alliances.

With adequate follow-up discussion, youth will gain a better understanding of the difficulties and complexities of nations agreeing and cooperating on different topics. Your group could also play this game at a retreat or camp.

FIND THE LEADERS

This fun game challenges your students to find their adult leaders in a large, crowded place. The adult leaders (or parents of youth in the group) hide in a mall, park, or other open area. The object of the game is for the youth to find as many of the leaders as they can in a set time.

The leaders should dress up in disguises to avoid being recognized. (But don't wear a ski-mask—that disguise will attract some unwanted attention!) The disguises can be as simple as ball caps, wigs, and glasses or as complex as fake facial hair, stage makeup for an aged look, a change of clothes, and costumes of the opposite sex.

If the adult leaders are driving the youth to the mall, the adults should drop the teens off at one end of the mall and have them stay in groups of at least three. The leaders then drive to the other end of the mall and change into costume. The volunteers will get some strange looks as they're slipping into character in the parking lot—especially if they're shaving off (or putting on) facial hair!

The leaders may wander the mall, go in and out of stores, eat at the food court, or just sit on a bench and read the newspaper. The only rule is that they can't hide in a restroom. They have to "hide" in plain sight.

When the youth find a leader, they receive a small token (such as a small piece of paper). The teens are to collect as many tokens as possible in the time allotted. Another option is to have each leader hand out a different token and challenge the youth to get one of each type of token. Or, instead of tokens, create a puzzle where each adult has a different piece and the youth attempt to put the entire puzzle together. Perhaps the puzzle contains a final destination where the youth should go for a special prize (such as the food court for an ice cream cone). Before the game, establish a meeting place and time for the group in case some youth don't get all of the pieces of the puzzle.

RIBBON SEARCH

The object of this game is for the group to find ribbons placed along a path or trail and follow them to a finish line or destination. Prior to the search, plan a route for your group to take, then tie small, colored ribbons to tree branches or bushes along that path. Do this part during the day, when you can easily find your way.

Later that night, have the group set out to find the ribbons. As the youth find ribbons, they should untie them and bring the ribbons with them to the final destination. Although the youth can play this game in daylight, it is more fun, challenging, and adventurous at night. To create an even bigger challenge, allow only one flashlight for the group.

To add another element to the game, include a Scripture verse on a piece of paper with each ribbon. One person from the group must memorize and recite the verse before the group can move on to the next ribbon. By the end, each person should have memorized one verse.

For a final destination or finish line, have the ribbons lead the group to an outlook point, outdoor chapel, cross atop a hill, or campfire circle for a devotion. If you are leading the group to a campfire setting, have materials for making S'Mores and roasting marshmallows.

FIND BARNEY

During the apex of a certain purple dinosaur's popularity, I received an eight-inch-tall stuffed Barney. The gift was anonymously left on my desk at work. When I approached my youth group about the purple monster, nobody claimed responsibility; but many kids laughed suspiciously. After exhausting all leads, I finally gave up and accepted my ownership of the little purple dino. So I decided to make the best of the situation and let everyone enjoy my new gift.

I took the toy and hid it in the rafters of the sanctuary. At first I was just curious to see if anyone would notice; I also wanted to see who was passing time during the sermon looking at the ceiling. It took a couple weeks, but some of the youth finally came to me and asked about Barney's new home in the rafters. My little experiment quickly grew into a weekly game of hide-and-seek. Every week I would relocate Barney to a new location in the church and the youth would try to find him. When planning this game, know that you don't have to tell the kids what's going on; just let them discover the game and join in on their own.

Also, you don't have to use Barney. Find something that your youth like or that holds a unique meaning for them. There's always some new character emerging in our pop culture, so if you're stuck, look for one. Remember that some pastors might not appreciate a stuffed toy migrating around the sanctuary and distracting the worship service. In that case, try using the youth room or the larger church building instead of the sanctuary.

Barney became a mascot for our group, and even parents started scanning the sanctuary for signs of purple. I never gave prizes for finding Barney, but you may choose to give a small reward to or keep a tally chart for those who find the object you've hidden. The reward could be that the first person to find the object gets to hide it the following week. Make sure to hide the object at a time when other people are not around.

OPTION FOR ANY GAME

If you're looking for a new aspect and teaching point to add to any game, try this option.

Youth who have not had physical limitations might have difficulty understanding what someone with a physical handicap faces day to day. To help those students in your group develop empathy, add the following aspects to any game the youth are playing:

• Tie one person's arm behind his or her back.

• Have one student sit in a wheelchair during the game.

• Blindfold one person and assign a guide to him or her.

• Assign one youth to act as if he or she were deaf and use only hand gestures to communicate to the group.

• Tie a youth's leg so that he or she must hop from place to place.

(Note: The youth can rely on help from their friends during the game.)

Carefully choose who has what limitation. Don't pick the quietest of the group to be deaf and mute—the other group members may not notice if he or she didn't talk! If you have a couple star athletes in the group who win every game of one-on-one basketball, blindfold them or tie their arms behind their backs. These limitations help level the playing field if the group is playing a competitive game. If you have group members who do have physical challenges, be sensitive to their feelings; you don't want them to feel that the other youth are making fun of them.

After the game is over, discuss how the game changed when some of the group members were faced with a handicap. Was the group annoyed that the game took longer? Were the youth who played deaf frustrated that they couldn't talk and that people didn't understand them? Did their friends get tired of helping? This game option can lead to a great discussion of how we are all important parts of the body of Christ, regardless of our physical abilities or inabilities. Or the game option can lead to a discussion about friendship and helping those in need, such as the time when a paralyzed man was lowered to Jesus through the roof of a building by four others (in Mark 2:3-4).

RETREATS AND TRIPS

CHRYSALIS AND OTHER THREE-DAY SPIRITUAL RETREATS

Founded in the Catholic tradition of Cursillo, Chrysalis is a three-day spiritual retreat that leads participants through the process of refocusing and renewal. Based on a caterpillar's transformation into a butterfly, the retreat allows the participants to enter as caterpillars and emerge from the chrysalis as butterflies. The theme of Chrysalis is "Die, Rise, Fly."

Chrysalis weekends are gender specific, so there are separate girls' and guys' weekends. Both follow the same curriculum and lead participants through a weekend where they experience the unconditional love of Christ.

Participants are placed in small groups and over the three days hear fifteen talks from adult and youth leaders on a variety of Christian development topics. Following each talk, the small groups have discussion and report back to the larger group. Other important parts of a Chrysalis weekend are prayer, worship, Communion, and guided personal reflection.

Chrysalis and other three-day spiritual retreats are not intended to be a conversion tool for nonbelievers or seekers but an opportunity for committed Christians to be nurtured and challenged to go deeper in their walk with God.

For more information, visit *www.upperroom.org/chrysalis*.

UNITED METHODIST SEMINARS

Many church denominations have unique opportunities that local youth workers never hear about. One that eluded me for ten years is United Methodist (UM) Seminars. This program equips high school and college-age youth with knowledge and hands-on, practical experience in a variety of topics and issues. And you don't have to be a United Methodist group to attend.

A local church taking a UM Seminars trip arranges a specific topic in advance with the leaders of the Seminars program. The seminars include topics such as environmental concerns; socioeconomic justice; the media; local, national, and international issues; race and racism; social holiness; child advocacy; and violence. Nearly any topic your group wants to study can be researched and presented in the seminars setting. The purpose of UM Seminars extends beyond just learning about a topic—the youth who attend can go out into the world and apply what they've learned.

The General Board of Church and Society of The United Methodist Church conducts the Seminars in New York City across the street from the United Nations, and in Washington D.C. on Capitol Hill in the United Methodist Building, located between the Supreme Court and US Capitol. The Seminars are inexpensive; your main expense is getting there.

UM Seminars is just one example of the educational and service opportunities available to youth workers and their groups. Check into the opportunities that your church denomination offers.

For more information about UM Seminars, visit *www.umc-gbcs.org/seminars/faq.php*.

SKI TRIP

Many companies organize ski trips for groups. And leaving the transportation, lodging, ski and snowboard rentals, and food arrangements to someone else is convenient. But if your budget doesn't allow for a packaged trip, here are some tips for planning a trip yourself:

- Ski or snowboard rentals and lift tickets do not have much flexibility in price other than group rates. So save money by finding alternative lodging, bringing food from home, and having parents or volunteers provide transportation.

- Instead of staying slope-side at an expensive resort, rent or borrow a family's cabin for the whole group. or stay at a nearby church; churches usually have a minimal fee for overnight stays and sometimes are free.

- The only place food is more expensive than at a professional sporting event is at the ski slopes. Save some money by trading in that six-dollar hot dog for a sack lunch. Plan the menu, purchase the food, and cook all of the meals yourself. If the thought of cooking for so many teens scares you, remember to keep it simple. Cereal, muffins, pastries, milk, and juice make for a simple breakfast anyone can prepare. Before leaving for the slopes, have the youth pack a sack lunch. With a PB-and-J sandwich, chips, an apple, and soda or juice, youth are set to go. For dinner, have a warm, hearty meal. Frozen lasagna, salad, bread, and milk or lemonade are always a crowd pleaser. For dessert, have cookies or brownies and ice cream.

- Chartering a bus is a luxurious way to travel, but it is also expensive. Save some money by renting vehicles or asking parents to drive. The vehicles should have seatbelts for everyone and enough room for luggage, food, and ski and snowboard equipment. Also make sure the church insurance company is on board. Then head to the slopes in a caravan of excited youth.

- Have any first-time skiers take a lesson before they ski on their own. Taking the lesson with your beginners will make them feel more comfortable. You may want to offer a non-skiing option for those who want to hang out in the lodge and stay warm; they make great helpers since they watch stuff, save a place for your group to meet, and prepare food.

- Be sure to contact the ski area you are visiting and ask about alternatives to downhill skiing. Many places have cross country skiing, snowshoeing, and tubing runs.

NIGHT OWL

Your teens will love a night-owl camp, retreat, or overnight. Owls are nocturnal, sleeping during the day and remaining active at night; and for this event, so will you.

This retreat or overnight is just like the ones the youth are use to, with one change: day becomes night, and night becomes day. Rearrange the schedule so that "morning" begins at sundown, and finish with "dinner" at sunrise. There's nothing like eggs and pancakes at 6:00 P.M. and hamburgers and hot dogs at 6:00 A.M. Schedule all of your activities to take place throughout the night. At bedtime, cover windows so that the group gets some sleep. Aluminum foil works well for keeping the sunshine at bay.

Conduct the camp, retreat, or overnight in the same way it would occur if it were happening at the regular time. This method will legitimize the event, and the youth will see it for more than a quirky gimmick. Go fishing, take a hike, go for a bike ride, kayak, canoe, play games outside, have guest speakers, and ring the meal bell for all to hear. Neighbors love that 11:00 P.M. lunch bell!

EVENTS

At first, this activity sounds disgusting to many people, and chances are your youth share that view. But if you can move beyond those initial apprehensions, the experience will bring your youth closer and set the tone of servanthood to which Christ calls us.

In John 13:1-9, Jesus washes the feet of the disciples. Simon Peter tells Jesus that he should wash Jesus' feet because Jesus is his teacher and master while he, Peter, is the student. Jesus explains to Peter that Christian leadership is based on serving others.

In the days of Jesus, servants customarily washed the feet of guests when the visitors entered a home. This practice involved cleaning feet with water and dressing them with oils and perfumes. When Jesus got on his hands and knees, he humbled himself and submitted to those he served, out of love for them. Jesus taught the disciples through his actions that they too should serve others in the same way.

Your youth may hesitate to participate in a foot-washing service because others' feet may be sweaty and smelly. If so, help the students imagine what foot washing was like in Jesus' time. People didn't wear socks and traveled along dirt roads and trails by foot, and since they bathed less frequently than we do, feet tended to get dirty, smelly, and rough. If feet are gross nowadays, imagine what they were like two thousand years ago in the hot, sandy desert."

For the foot-washing ritual, place a pitcher of water (add foot powder to the water to prevent the spread of germs), a stack of towels, and a basin on the floor in front of a chair. Pour water into the basin and invite the group to enter into worship through the service of foot washing. If your youth are divided by junior and senior high, you might want to take different approaches:

- **For senior high**—Invite the youth to come forward in pairs. Have one person sit while the other washes his or her feet, then ask them to switch and repeat the washing. For each pair of feet, provide a clean towel and discard it into a separate pile. You may provide a mild perfume, powder, or lotion to be rubbed on feet after the washing. When a pair of youth complete their washing, they return to their seats and the next pair takes its turn. Have the youth pray silently or aloud for the person receiving the foot washing as they await their turn

- **For junior high**—Invite the youth to come one by one as they feel led. As you wash each student's feet, tell him or her how special he or she is. Pray for each student by name, and vow to serve each one in any way you can.

Try to achieve a reverent tone for the foot-washing service. You can expect occasional giggles and sighs, since the youth will probably find this ritual new. But remind the group that this ritual is a prayerful, respectful offering to God and one another. When setting the tone, you may consider lighting candles, playing music, or having complete silence during the service.

The setting for a foot washing service is less important than the tone. However, if you want a great place for this service, try the living room or family room of a home, since the story from John 13 takes place in an intimate room. The service also works in a sanctuary, youth room, hallway, or outdoor location.

A foot-washing service makes for a powerful experience for any group, no matter what size. Hearing water wash over feet and splash into the basin as youth pray for one another symbolizes Christ's servantlike love washing over each member of the group. Feeling Christ's love together in this way will help the group grow closer. Use this tool on its own, on retreats, as leadership training, as part of a New Year's Eve covenant service, or in whatever way meets your needs. The ritual will definitely leave a lasting memory in the faith lives of your students.

ADVENTURE AND DESTINATION-UNKNOWN DAYS

Fun anytime of the year, adventure days are the perfect summertime memory maker. Plan a weekly outing for your group by designating a specific day adventure day. This event is similar to destination-unknown outings, except you can tell your youth where they'll be going each week.

When planning adventure days, look for things to do at local attractions. For example, if you live in Seattle, go to Pike Place Market to watch flying fish, or go up in the Space Needle. It's amazing how many local people rarely do the "tourist" things in their home cities. Keep in mind that most teens (and adults) can't afford to spend lots of money every week. So plan a mix of free and low-cost activities. Also plan a variety of adventures to appeal to the diverse interests of your group.

Here are some examples of adventure day activities:

- Take a boat or ferry ride.
- Go to the zoo.
- Rollerblade in a park.
- Go swimming.
- Go to a museum.
- See an IMAX movie.
- Take a bike ride.
- Hike to a fun destination.
- Go window shopping in a big city or expensive store.
- Visit a historical site or monument.
- Take a tour of a local industry such as a candy shop or an ice cream factory.
- Go to a local festival or fair

For destination-unknown outings, let the youth know what time they'll be back, if they need to bring anything, and how much the event will cost. Then surprise them with the destination. Look for great Destination Unknown ideas in *Destination Unknown: 50 Quick Mystery Trips for Youth Groups*, by Sam Halverson. ISBN 0-687-09724-X.

YOUTH SUNDAY

(Note: If worship occurs on a different day in your church, simply substitute the name of the appropriate day of the week for the word *Sunday*.)

Have you ever wondered what Sunday mornings would look like if the youth group were responsible for worship? The youth would probably sleep in until 11:30 A.M. then roll out of bed around noon. While this situation isn't exactly what Youth Sunday means, Sunday morning will probably look and feel a little different, since youth will take the reins and lead worship.

Youth-led worship means more than designating youth as ushers and Scripture readers (a practice that should already be happening). The youth group conducts and leads every aspect of worship. Communion and baptism aside, youth make announcements, lead prayers, read Scripture, teach the children's lesson, play and sing music, preach the sermon, usher, and greet.

With the pastor, select a Sunday when the youth group will lead worship. The youth can either lead a typical service in which they simply replace the pastor and style of worship. This second option usually reflects youth better, allowing them to invest themselves more fully in the service. This worship style can also be a source of consternation for older members of the church: The music may be too loud or fast for them, and they may think the youth don't dress "correctly." But usually members are not only gracious but truly delighted to see the youth in leadership.

With support from church leadership, this day provides a chance to introduce new elements into worship and highlight youths' gifts. Drama, dance, painting, poetry, and song all bring a new spin to traditional worship elements. A youth band can lead the worship music by singing songs that are sung at youth group instead of the regular hymns and choruses. Instead of preaching from the pulpit, the teens might bring a couch up from the youth room and sit on it as they discuss the message. Encourage the youth to design a worship service they like and to share their way of worshiping with others in the congregation.

Look for youth worship resources for a starting point in planning. (Check out the *Worship Feast* resources at *www.ileadyouth.com*.) Encourage the students to write prayers and blessings for the service.

ALTERNATIVE PROM

Prom is an exciting event for high school students, unless the person they were waiting to ask or be asked by decides to ask, or is asked by, someone else. While happy thoughts usually surround prom, it can be a devastating time of year for many teens. Some youth never get asked to prom, and others are too shy to ask someone on a date. Some can't afford the multi-hundred-dollar event that prom has become, while others are too self-conscious about their weight, looks, finances, height, or social status. And some just aren't interested in dressing up and making a big deal out of the evening.

Here's a fun way to turn prom into an evening to remember for those who would like to forget prom altogether: Host an alternative prom at your church! You don't have a date for this prom because you don't need one. You might establish a rule that you can't have a date.

Schedule the Alternative Prom on the same night as the school's prom, and send invitations to the youth group. Decorate a room at the church, hanging streamers, balloons, signs, and string lights. You might ask parents to provide a nice dinner where they serve youth, bring in fast food, or order in pizza. After supper, it's dance time. Hire a DJ to play music, or have everyone bring an appropriate CD from home. Turn the lights down and turn up the music, but limit the slow songs, because these teens are the youth who don't have dates.

For dress code, publicize "dress down" or "come as you are." This dress code allows youth to attend without

making them feel that they have to buy or rent something expensive. If your group wants to dress up but doesn't want to go to prom, have them wear the fancy clothes to dinner and then change for the rest of the evening.

Some other great ideas to make this evening more special are to
- give each person a plastic flower corsage or boutonniere when he or she arrives
- have an instant or digital camera for group photos
- conduct a drawing for cool prizes (such as popsicles)
- dress up like a chauffeur and drive the church van to dinner
- show a video or go to the theater for a movie
- make the prom an overnight with separate girls' and guys' rooms for sleeping
- come up with a theme (such as '70s, '80s, or pirates).

Your youth will remember this evening for years to come. It affirms teenagers for who they are and doesn't judge them based on their date-ability. It keeps them from being left out simply because they don't have the money or a date to go to prom. And everyone has a "prom" experience to relay the next day. And who knows?—with community support, this event could become more popular than the school's prom.

CHAPERONE A SCHOOL FUNCTION

Here's a way for you to make memories with youth on their turf: Contact your teens' schools and volunteer to chaperone at school dances and class parties whenever needed. Schools are always looking for help with chaperoning, and many schools have a calling list for when they need more assistance. But most schools are looking for any help they can get. If you volunteer, chances are you'll get a call in no time.

Chaperoning a dance or trip will show kids you care, and they'll be touched that you wanted to be there. Plus, they will love having you around, because they consider you cooler than their parents and teachers. You'll be surprised at how many youth introduce you to their friends; they'll want to show you off!

You'll also get to know school administrators, teachers, and staff. Now you'll have a point of reference when your students talk to you about their days at school.

CHAUFFEUR A GROUP OF YOUTH TO A SCHOOL DANCE

Make lasting memories by volunteering to chauffeur a group of youth to a school dance. Many youth can't afford to rent a limousine; this way, they don't have to feel bad about not shelling out the bucks for one. This idea also works well for youth who do not have a driver's license, do not have access to a car, live in states with teenage driving restrictions (such as no other passengers except family), but don't want their parents driving them to the school dance. And the parents may feel more comfortable with you as the chauffeur than if the youth were driving themselves.

Before the night of the dance, make reservations at a restaurant. The night of the dance, dress up and play the part of chauffeur. A white shirt, dark pants, jacket, cap, and a bow tie will make you look more authentic. Borrowing or renting a nice car for a day will add to the experience, but any car will work. Place a couple of the teens' favorite sodas in a small cooler in the back seat.

Pick up your "clients" at their houses and allow time for the parents to take pictures of the youth. Then take the youth to the restaurant. Drive up to the front door, stop, get out, and open the car door for them. Then wait in the parking lot for them. (This period is a great time to read a book, work on a laptop, or make cell phone calls.) When the youth come out of the restaurant, drive up to the front door, get out and once again open the doors for them.

Now it's off to the dance. Repeat the door routine when dropping youth off at the dance. Arrange to pick them up at the end of the dance, so that you can go home before that time. Make sure they have your phone number if they need to get a hold of you sooner. Following the dance, either drop youth off at another restaurant for dessert or take them home.

Stay in character the entire time you are with them, since you are their chauffeur and not their parent, babysitter, or youth leader. Always address them as "sir" and "ma'am," tip your hat, and act like a real chauffeur would. This chauffeur service will help kids out and make their dance a little more special.

If you want to include more youth, use the church van as the limo.

FAST-FOOD FORMAL DINNER

Whoever said you have to eat your burger and fries from a wrapper or cardboard carton? No law prohibits a nice table setting in fast-food restaurants. Provide this fun dining experience to the whole group, to a small group of couples on a date, before a school dance, special occasions such as Valentine's Day, or just for fun. Fast-food formal dinners make great substitutes for expensive dinners at fancy restaurants. Contact the manager of a local fast-food restaurant, and arrange a special dinner on the town for your youth group. Your group doesn't have to know where they are going for dinner, just that they need to dress nicely and bring ten bucks. Or instead of keeping the destination a secret, tell the kids where they will be eating and let them have fun with the thought of fine dining on fast food.

Arrange to have volunteers, parents, or youth workers at the restaurant to serve as the host, the servers, and the concierge. The volunteers should prepare the tables by setting them with tablecloths, place mats, stone plates, glasses, silverware, napkins, and centerpieces such as flowers. If you bring candles, check with the restaurant before lighting them.

As the youth arrive, the host should meet them at the door and ask how many are in their party, guide them to their table, and seat them. Youth should be treated as they would be at a five-star restaurant but without the cost. After everyone is seated, the servers should mention any specials (such as a value meal) and take orders. You can make menus to hand out, but the youth will know the basic menu because they've probably eaten at the restaurant many times. Writing the orders down will help keep everything straight when servers stand in line at the counter. When food is ready, the servers should deliver it to the tables while holding up the trays like real waiters and waitresses.

Have the volunteers refill drinks and bring extra ketchup, napkins, and salt to the tables as needed. When the youth finish eating, clear their dishes and follow the same ordering-and-serving procedure for dessert. After the entire meal, load up and head back to the church.

Here's another twist on a fast-food formal dinner: Set up card tables and chairs in a park, on a street corner, on the steps of city hall, at the beach, or anywhere you want; and have your fast-food fine dining in public. Dress up nicely, set the table, and have fun. If people travel to France for sidewalk-café dining, why not enjoy the same experience in your town at a fraction of the cost?

GUEST SPEAKER SERIES

Talking about any topic with youth is sometimes a battle of attention spans. As the leader, you want the youth to listen and hear the message. At the same time, they quickly lose interest if they don't have a good reason to listen. Nobody is an expert in every area, and a lack of new information to relay to the teens can result in shorter-than-planned lessons.

To add variety to your youth program and keep the attention of your students, bring in guest speakers. Whether for a single lesson or a series of lessons, a guest speaker who is familiar with the topic will keep the youth interested. For example, you may know a lot about the conflict between Israel and Palestine but can't relay the perspective of someone who has lived there. Youth are interested in real, tangible stories and experiences. Perceived as more authoritative, guest speakers bring a legitimacy to a topic, causing youth to invest themselves more fully in the lesson.

Here are some other ideas for guest speakers:

• Instead of just talking to youth about the dangers that come with drug use, bring in a police officer who has served as an undercover drug dealer.

• Instead of just talking about the risks of sex, bring in a single parent or someone with AIDS to relate his or her story.

• Instead of just talking about war, bring in someone who has served in the military.

• Instead of just talking about the poor, abused, or homeless, bring in a person who works on the front lines of these issues.

• Instead of just discussing the importance of missions, bring in a missionary to share his or her story.

These real-life experiences will keep youth interested, invested, and focused.

If a topic is too extensive to cover in one youth group meeting, plan a series of guest speakers. And if the topic is controversial, plan a series of guest speakers who represent the differing views on the topic. With a balanced approach, youth get a larger picture of the issues and are given the tools to think objectively about the topic. If appropriate, invite the parents to part of or all of the guest speakers' presentations. If your topic is highly controversial, make sure your parents are well-informed about what their kids are going to be discussing.

OUTDOOR CINEMA

Remember the days of drive-in movies? A few of those places are still around, but most youth have never been to one. If you don't have one near you but want a similar experience, try creating an outdoor cinema.

You'll need a projector, VCR, or DVD player and a large screen (a white bed sheet works well). Hang the sheet on an outside wall of your church, and project the movie onto the homemade screen.

Since most projectors put out a limited sound volume, you might want to use speakers so that everyone can hear the movie. With four speakers, you can create stereo surround sound (which beats a small metal box hanging from the inside of your window).

Let the youth bring their youth room couches, chairs, pillows, bean bags, and blankets outside to sit on. Those blankets come in handy on a cool evening. Provide popcorn and other snacks (you can set up a vending booth), or have the kids bring snacks from home.

Have fun choosing movies your group will like. Some groups prefer old Godzilla movies with poorly synchronized dubbing, while others like state-of-the-art special effects. One of the best movies for youth groups is *The Princess Bride*, because it is so quotable and contains only one bad word. Plenty of movies have great morals and messages for young people, and you know your group better than anyone else, so chose an appropriate movie for your group. Never underestimate the popularity of computer-animated vegetables!

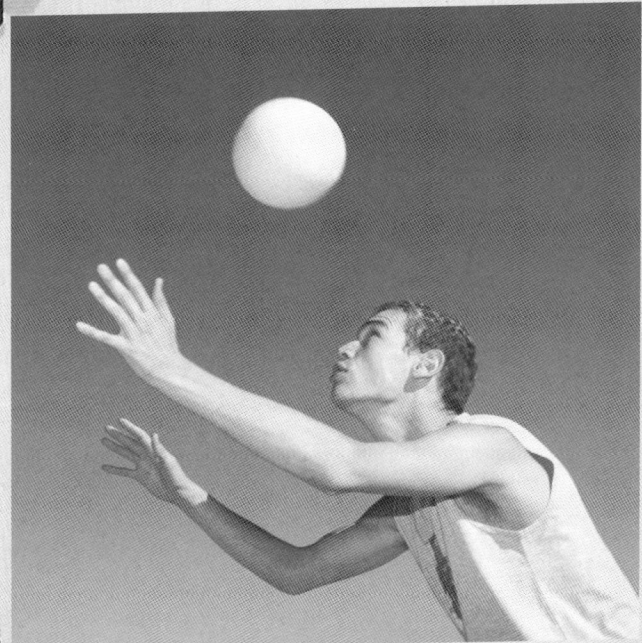

VARIATIONS OF A PROGRESSIVE DINNER

Traditional progressive dinners begin at one location and move to another, then to another, and so forth. At each location, a different course is served. Have appetizers at the first house, salad at the second, a main course at the third, and dessert at the final house. (You may want to ask the youths' parents if they would host a segment of a meal at their houses.) One variation is to have only one part of the main course at each house. The youth will likely find this option fun, because they get to visit more homes of their fellow group members.

If you don't have time to go from house to house, try having a progressive dinner in your church. Instead of homes, use different rooms in the church, allowing the youth to travel from course to course. This option fits well into an open house event for your entire church. After your church has completed a building expansion or remodeling, host a progressive dinner that serves as a tour of your new facilities.

An option that saves parents from having to do dishes is a fast-food progressive dinner. Take a survey of the youth group and determine which fast-food establishment has the best appetizer, fries, onion rings, burger or sandwich, milkshake, and dessert. Take the results of the survey and plan a progressive dinner that visits each place for its respective favorite item. It's fun to see the reactions of restaurant employees when a group walks in and orders the same item for each person in the group, such as fifteen small fries.

For service or outreach progressive dinner, collect canned food and other "dinner" items from different members of your church. As with a traditional progressive dinner, the youth will travel from house to house. Instead of eating at each house, they will collect one type of food: canned vegetables at the first house, bread at the second, a boxed main course (such as macaroni and cheese) at the third, and a boxed dessert (cake, brownies, or cookies) at the fourth. Be sure to advertise that the youth group is doing this activity and that church members should expect a visit on a specific date. See how many complete dinners your group can put together for a local food bank. If your group is large, divide it into smaller groups and go to different houses. This arrangement will involve more homes and increase the number of members from the church who will have a chance to contribute.

CHRISTIAN MUSIC FESTIVALS

Each summer, regions around the United States have large Christian music festivals. These multi-day events in the tradition of Woodstock include talented Christian speakers and bands. With creative names like Jesus Jams, King Fest, Spirit Song, and Creation, these events draw Christian groups together for an awesome time of corporate prayer, praise, worship, and fellowship.

Most of these festivals are held in venues with overnight camping and RV facilities. Unfortunately, most do not have shower facilities. But that disadvantage won't stop the youth from having a great time. Concerts and speakers typically start mid-morning and run late into the night. Some festivals have interactive venues such as skate parks, opportunities to meet the bands, autograph sessions, and support groups.

To save money, bring food and drinks to avoid the marked-up prices at the festival. A barbeque grill is one of the best investments you can make for a trip like this one. Festival-goers commonly bring tents to sleep in, but some groups rent RVs. The biggest advantage to an RV is its private restroom. Just make sure the site has dump station facilities; otherwise your restroom will fill quickly and become unusable. The cost for festival entrance varies, but these events usually offer a group discount.

Visit www.christianconcerts.com to search for Christian music festivals in your area. Even if you have to drive a day or two to get there, the event will be worth it! One last bit of advice: Bring lots of ice, drinking water, sunscreen, and bug spray!

MIDNIGHT KAYAKING, CANOEING, OR TUBING

Youth and adults alike enjoy gliding across the water in a canoe or sea kayak. Different from white water kayaks, sea kayaks are similar to canoes and come in one- or two-person models. If canoes or kayaks aren't available, a slow float in an inner tube is always fun.

A lake, bay, or slow-moving river is ideal for this outdoor activity. (Make sure all participants wear life vests and are instructed on water safety.) Floating on the water is fun in itself and provides the perfect venue for a lesson on creation, the environment, or stewardship of natural resources. Explore the shoreline, grass and lily pad fields, marsh land, and other interesting aspects of the area. The water is often clear enough to see fish swimming below the surface.

To make this activity more memorable, try venturing out after sundown. Waiting for dark and being away from light pollution will provide an unprecedented view of the heavens. Being on the water under a sky full of stars will make an impression on youth that will last for years. You might also plan your midnight kayaking or canoeing trip to coincide with a meteor shower. One of the most active of these showers is the summer's Perseid meteor shower.

Another unique phenomenon found in some regions is phosphorescence. As a kayak or canoe cuts through the water, it stirs single-celled algae, causing a chemical reaction within the algae that makes the wake coming off of the boat glow. This whitish glow can also be seen coming from the swirls created when a paddle is pulled through the water.

Although fun during daylight hours, kayaking or canoeing at night with a light show above and below can be a completely new experience for youth.

30 HOUR FAMINE

Have your youth ever gone thirty consecutive hours without eating? Probably not. If they are typical teens, it's more likely that they've eaten for thirty consecutive hours. So invite them to try the 30 Hour Famine, an annual hunger awareness and fundraising fast sponsored by World Vision. It gives youth a chance to go hungry and expand their knowledge about world hunger issues.

Starting on Friday, participants fast for thirty straight hours, which end on Saturday evening. During this time, youth participate in Bible study, activities, lessons, and outreach service projects. World Vision provides curriculum resources for groups registered to participate in the 30 Hour Famine.

A preferred way of conducting the famine is to have an overnight at the church where youth can support one another through the experience. This arrangement also allows your group to grow in their understanding of the need that exists in the world and at the same time have an introduction to the spiritual discipline of fasting.

During the famine, have the youth examine how much money their family spends on groceries each week. Working at a food bank or soup kitchen and seeing hungry people makes the experience even more real for students.

Officially conducted the final weekend in February, the 30 Hour Famine can be done anytime during the year. For more information about the 30 Hour Famine, go to *www.30hourfamine.org*.

CHAPTER 2
FAMILY, GENDER-SPECIFIC, AND INTERGENERATIONAL ACTIVITIES

Helping your youth make real connections with their church, their families, and their peers will make lasting memories. This chapter's ideas celebrate family, utilize the uniqueness of gender-specific activities, and bridge the gap between generations.

Youth usually dread their parents being at youth group (or anywhere within five miles of their friends). The ideas in this chapter celebrate their differences and allow youth and parents to see each other in a different light. The ideas will encourage laughter and open the door to deeper friendships.

As teenagers, youth are fully charged with hormones and take interest in the opposite sex. If your youth group is typical, it has at least one guy who attends because the girls are cute or one girl who attends because the guys are hot. This situation is why sometimes gender-specific activities work

better than co-ed ones. Getting together as just guys or as just girls can help your youth move beyond superficial discussions to honest dialogue on certain topics.

Youth have a distorted idea of the word *old*. (You know this fact if you're over thirty.) Recently a youth I know pointed out that a particular pair of boots "weren't for old people—you know, people over twenty-five." So just imagine how old seventy or eighty must seem to them.

Use this chapter's ideas for intergenerational connection, which will help the students discover that older adults aren't the dinosaurs the kids had once thought. And at the same time, the older adults will learn that your teens aren't the unruly bunch they thought the teens were.

FAMILY

DECADE SWITCH

Does it make you feel old when youth ask what you wore in high school because they need ideas for their school's retro dance? Well, here's a fun idea the teens and their parents will both enjoy: a decade switch.

Plan a party for the youth and their parents. The twist is that to attend the party, the teens and the parents have to switch decades. That's right—youth dress as their parents did in high school, and parents dress as their youth do today. Depending on current fashion trends, this party can be scarier for parents than for youth.

During the party, have a fashion show or costume contest where each age group rates the other. The parents choose the most authentic retro costume, and youth choose the most authentic up-to-date costume. The judges might also award fun prizes for best and worst dressed, funniest dressed, most realistic, biggest bell bottoms, and so forth.

Another option for a decade switch is to choose a decade and have everyone dress in the same era. Choose a decade that has potential for fun costumes and is foreign to both groups, such as the twenties.

In addition to dressing up, play music from the selected decades and highlight any trends or fads from that era. To create more atmosphere, find a record player and (if one of the decades is the sixties or seventies) an eight-track player. Have the parents and the youth bring music. It's also fun to have parents bring photos or yearbooks from decades past and to browse through those memorabilia.

FAMILY MISSION TRIP

Mission trips, fun and meaningful experiences, allow youth groups to bond. But family mission trips bring your youth group together and help families grow closer. Such trips can transform your youth group, their families, and your church. You know the benefits youth gain from a mission trip. Imagine these benefits extending to the family members of the teens.

You'll need to have appropriate mission work for all ages, from children to grandparents. Everyone should feel as though he or she contributes and has a role in the trip's success. Mission trips should combine spiritual sharing, physical labor, and Christian fellowship. Tap into the strengths of your families to maximize effectiveness in each area.

Children can participate in local activities such as a vacation Bible school, arts and crafts, or jamboree program. Youth and adults can help implement those programs and assist in repair or construction projects. Parents can bond with their children and teach the youth practical carpentry and other building skills.

Plan some fellowship and worship opportunities that include all ages. A large meal together is a perfect way to have fellowship with local families. Provide all of the food, or have a potluck dinner and enjoy the tastes of local cuisine. Follow the meal with a worship service.

If you have some students whose parents do not attend the church, encourage them to invite their parents. If that request is not feasible, ask a family or adult mentor to be the teen's family for the trip.

Lodging: Look for a campground with cabins or dorms near your mission location. Tent camping with showers nearby also works. A family could bring its RV if it has one.

Food: If you don't have designated cooks, divide all of the participants into kitchen teams. These groups rotate in preparing and serving food and cleaning up following the meals.

Plan for evening devotions, singing, and campfires. Have families sign up to lead devotions, or have youth design the evening programs.

Make sure you also have some plain old good times around the campfire with S'Mores and the like. You may ask each family to tell a funny story about itself. If you have older adults on the trip, invite them to give a testimony or say what their hopes and dreams are for the youth.

MOTHER-DAUGHTER DAY

Help your girls reconnect with their moms with a lunch-and-shopping day. Go to a restaurant and send each pair to a table for two. Give them some questions to talk about, and have them pray together. After lunch, go shopping, see a show, or go to the zoo. If you have girls who would rather go skiing or camping, adapt the day to fit your group. If you have girls whose mothers are unavailable, assign a mentor to them so that those girls are included.

If you're a male youth leader, send a female volunteer to coordinate this one! Any way you conduct this day, take lots of pictures for the scrapbooks.

FAMILY BIBLE STUDIES

Support the parents of your students by offering a short-term Bible study for the whole family. Include topics such as handling stress, dealing with people who are different from you, and loving your neighbor. Play some family-building games to strengthen your students' relationships at home, and offer some time for parents to listen to their teens and vice versa.

One option is to hold the session on a weeknight in the summer. Summer is often a time to offer some programs and studies that are different from your school year planning. Order pizza or subs, and eat together. The parents will love the opportunity to spend time with their teens, since the family may be too busy at home to sit down and reconnect. They'll love you for scheduling this time into their weeks (although receiving that appreciation is not why you have Bible study).

FATHER-SON GETAWAY

Dads will love this chance to get away and bond with their sons. Plan a trip that meets the needs of your group. You may have skiers, hunters, campers, or even shoppers. Try whatever the fathers and sons would enjoy the most. If you have some guys whose fathers are not in town or are unavailable, assign a mentor to each of them.

While you're on the day trip, designate some one-on-one time for dads and sons and for mentors and guys. Give them some questions to discuss, and encourage them to pray together.

If you're a female youth leader, you'll want to send one of your male volunteers on this one. Don't forget to take pictures!

GENDER SPECIFIC

GIRLS' OR GUYS' NIGHT OUT

It's time for the girls and guys to get out on their own for a night. Without the distraction of the opposite sex, the youth will get to know one another better and focus on their similarities instead of competing for attention.

You can use girls' or guys' night out as an outreach tool for inviting new youth to your group. Lots of teens are intimidated by the thought of visiting a group of people they don't know. Knowing that the group is all girls or all guys takes a little of the fear away, because everyone already has something in common.

The night out can be done on different levels, depending on the dynamics of your group. If your youth are young and don't know one another well, plan a fun evening with low-pressure activities. The youth should feel free to join in without feeling pressure to participate. Go shopping, do a group scavenger hunt, or rent movies and provide pop popcorn for some fun fellowship activities.

If your group is older and the youth are close, plan an evening that includes more specific activities you know your kids will like or new activities they might be willing to try. Youth who know one another well will be more comfortable participating in something new.

Although a night out can easily be done in one evening, an overnight lock-in adds to the fun. For more variety, have an outing (such as bowling or a movie) earlier in the evening with an overnight later at the church, where kids can stay up and bond.

For a deeper experience, make the gender-specific event a retreat. With just girls or guys, you'll have a chance to deepen the experience. Instead of merely doing "fun" activities, plan some activities that help your group connect through more intimate bonding. Worship and prayer will be meaningful and unique with a close-knit group of girls or guys.

Whether you make the girls' or guys' time a retreat or a one-night event, consider including parents as chaperones. This way, the parents and their children can just hang out as girls or as guys and have fun. Encourage the parents to be participants instead of, well, parents.

If you have both a girls' and a guys' night out, make those times a week apart. Bring a video camera so that you can tape all of the fun. You could have each group make a video for the opposite group; after both nights are complete, show both videos to the whole youth group. You'll get lots of laughs as the youth relive their special nights out. These tapes also serve as a great advertisement for those who weren't there. Seeing how much fun the night out was, those kids won't want to miss the next one.

GUYS PLAN THE GIRLS' NIGHT

For a twist on the girls' night out, have the guys plan the night for them. Have them choose the games, movies, activities, and so forth. The guys choose the menu and cook the meal. You could even have them serve the meal and clean up.

If you choose, the guys could be tour guides for the evening. As organizers of the event, they could take the girls to any restaurant, sights, or events the guys choose (within reason). They should send the fliers, organize adult volunteers, decide how much the event costs, and so forth. Have your guys put a lot of thought into planning a fun night for the girls.

GIRLS PLAN THE GUYS' NIGHT

Follow the same procedure as "Guys Plan a Girls' Night," only have the girls plan the night this time.

GIRLS' OR GUYS' BIBLE STUDY

As with the girls' or guys' night out, this Bible study moves youth into a serious study of God's Word without the distractions of the opposite sex. This isn't to say that Bible study with mixed genders doesn't work; a single-sex group just provides a different dynamic that allows for a different style of study.

Guys and girls face many similar challenges and issues, but they also have ones unique to their gender. Or, at the very least, they approach challenges differently. In a gender-specific Bible study, you'll be able to approach these challenges and issues from a shared perspective. For example, a guys' discussion on dating or friends will probably be differ considerably from a girls'.

A gender-specific Bible study also creates a different feeling of trust, support, and accountability. With a close group, youth will feel more comfortable discussing issues and are more likely to seek guidance and advice from adult leaders in times of need or crisis.

To create an even different dynamic and purpose to the Bible study, invite the parents to join the group. A father-son or mother-daughter Bible study is an activity youth and parents will appreciate for a lifetime.

D-GROUPS: DISCIPLESHIP AND ACCOUNTABILITY GROUPS

Discipleship groups are small groups that meet outside the church at least every other week. With an adult leader and four to six youth of the same sex and a similar age, D-groups provide an opportunity for teens to grow closer through fellowship. D-groups can meet at someone's house, at a park, in a coffee shop, inside a mall, or anywhere the group desires.

D-groups have several purposes, but the main purpose is to provide an opportunity for youth to develop intimate friendships while growing closer to God. D-groups have a variety of curriculum options; some ideas are listed below. At the minimum, D-groups should include a devotional and prayer at each meeting.

D-groups can focus on Bible study, service, outreach, missions, or any part of our Christian calling. D-groups often meet for social, recreational, or service activities and share in Christian fellowship while doing so. The most effective D-groups combine all three with outreach and study. A variety of activities provide a well-rounded approach to helping kids connect with one another.

Take your D-group to volunteer at a soup kitchen or a shelter for battered persons. Get together and watch the latest playoff game. Bake cookies in the church kitchen, or go bowling. There is no limit to what D-groups can do. On occasion, arrange for all of the D-groups to do an activity together. Or make a D-group competition between groups. For example, challenge each D-group to collect more canned food than the other groups for a canned food drive, offering a special prize for the D-group that collects the most.

In addition to serving others, D-groups increase participation in youth ministry, since group members invite other youth to join their D-group. Many youth find it daunting to visit a youth group where twenty or more people they don't know are staring at them. Since it is less intimidating to join and make friends in a group of four to six, D-groups are the perfect way to involve newcomers.

Since D-groups should have few members, they split to form two new groups after they reach eight to ten people. The two new D-groups invite more youth to join, and they start building again. D-groups should not become too big and lose the intimacy they were created to develop. Make sure D-groups don't become cliquish groups of individuals; members should be open and kind to others. If a D-Group is closed to others, it isn't a D-group but a clique. Here are some resources for Discipleship Groups:

- *Synago, 3V Bible Studies*, and *LinC* (For more information, go to *ileadyouth.com*.)

- *Devo'Zine* (For more information, call 1-800-925-6847.)

INTERGENERATIONAL

ADOPT-A-GRANDPARENT

This program effectively brings youth and older members of your church or community together. Obvious gaps exist between these generations, but an Adopt-a-Grandparent program provides an easy way to pull them together. For our purposes, a grandparent is any older adult. Grandparents need not have biological children or grandchildren to participate in this program.

Some youth are fortunate to know their grandparents, but many either never knew their grandparents or live too far away to have a face-to-face relationship with them. At the same time, many older adults feel alone and long for companionship. An Adopt-a-Grandparent program matches youth with elderly persons to help fill the void in each others' lives. The youth might think they have nothing to learn from or can't relate to a "grandparent" type, but they'll soon learn otherwise.

This ongoing program can run congruent with other youth activities and doesn't have to replace your normal youth group meetings. After explaining the program to your church, have youth and older adults sign up for "adoption." Create a biographical information sheet for all participants to fill out. Students who are searching for a grandparent to adopt can look at the information on grandparents. In addition to basic name, address, and phone number, good questions for the grandparent bio include:

- What are your likes and dislikes?
- What are your hobbies?
- Are you employed?
- Do you volunteer anywhere?
- What have you done for a living?
- What do you do in your free time?
- What are some of your favorite things (movies, color, food, music)?
- Do you have children, grandchildren, or great grandchildren?

Include any other questions you feel would help youth in knowing a little about each grandparent. Once a youth has chosen or been assigned a grandparent, send the youth bio to the grandparent with a letter explaining they will be contacted by the youth.

Youth should commit to contacting their grandparent at least once a week by a phone call, letter, e-mail, or visit. They should also plan on spending time in person with their grandparents at least twice a month. After fulfilling these minimum requirements, the youth may be as active as they want.

Now that youth are paired up with grandparents, what do they do? That's up to each pair to decide. Much of the contact will depend on the mobility, schedule, and energy level of each participant. Have the youth consult the bio sheets or ask their grandparents what they like to do when planning a get-together. They can play cards, go for a walk, have a meal together, go shopping, make scrapbooks, or whatever they're interested in doing. Even homework is a great activity—a former Spanish or math teacher makes a great tutor!

Let the youth know they are not "entertainment" for their grandparents and don't have to prepare something to do every time they visit. Many times, older people just want someone to talk with.

Some teens think older adults are inactive, go-to-bed-early types who don't leave the house much. And many older people think youth are shallow, unappreciative consumers who can't see beyond themselves. Through an Adopt-a-Grandparent program, both groups will quickly learn they couldn't be more wrong. The youth and the older adults will find the treasures that lie within each other through this mentoring program.

P.S. Watch out for some of those grandparents—they can be more wild than youth!

E-MAIL CLASSES

One reason older adults feel disconnected from young people is the pace of these youngsters' lives. Teens live in a much faster world than when older adults were growing up. A major reason things are faster nowadays, technology intimidates many older adults, who shy away from it, thinking they can't do activities it involves.

To bridge the technology gap and get youth connected with older members of the community, have your youth give them e-mail classes. Many teens use e-mail every day and almost never think twice about how to do it, because it comes so naturally to them. Who better to teach others about e-mail than those who are proficient?

The biggest challenge in developing this intergenerational outreach is the logistics of a facility. If your church has a computer lab, logistics aren't an issue. If you don't have a computer lab at your church, you can create one by having church members donate their older computers when they replace them with newer ones. (Remember that you'll need to have Internet access for all of those computers.) If this arrangement is not an option in your church, here are some other ideas that might work:

- Check with schools and libraries that have computer facilities to see if they are willing to host e-mail classes.

- Many retirement communities, senior centers, and assisted-living facilities have installed computer stations or classrooms for their members. Contact those facilities and arrange to have youth lead a class or series of classes on e-mail.

For the classes, offer training for a range of abilities, from beginner to more experienced. Cover everything from turning on the computer to printing, scanning, attaching files, and downloading digital photos. These aspects may sound extremely basic, but remember that some of these people will be sitting at a computer for the first time in their lives.

Give your youth some tips on teaching before their first time in front of a class. Remind them to speak slowly, clearly, and loud enough for everyone to hear. They should also pause frequently to see if there are any questions or comments.

These e-mail classes will empower older adults to reach out to family and friends through a new medium. The youths' lessons will not only help bridge the technology gap but will also help bridge the generation gap between older adults and youth.

PROM REVISITED

Do your youth ever wonder what their parents, grandparents, or other members of your church were like when they were in high school? Here's a chance for the teens to take a trip back in time and get a glimpse of high school life in the good ol' days. This event will also give older adults a chance to relive their glory days.

Have the youth group host a prom dance for the older adults of the church. Choose whether to set a minimum age for participants. If you want this event to include grandparents, make the minimum age fifty or fifty-five; if you want to include the parents of the youth, drop the minimum age to thirty-five or so. If you want a mix of all ages, forgo the minimum age requirement and let everyone participate.

Send invitations, sell tickets, or just have an open door to the Prom Revisited. Invite persons individually. Make sure people know they don't have to have a date to attend. The attendance at the event will be better with this extra effort. Be clear about the expectations for dressing up. With "prom" as the name for the event, some older couples may not come if they feel they must invest in fancy clothes. You may wish to downplay dressing up. At least communicate the evening's "dress code."

Decorate a room at the church, provide snacks, and play music from the eras represented. (Big Band music is popular and easy to find.) If you need help finding music, ask the participants bring any music from that era that they would like played.

To add a bit of fun to the festivities, have a dance exhibition. Youth may know the latest dance craze, but can they shimmy? Let those fleet-of-foot older members show off their moves as they dance the Charleston, the twist, or the hustle. Let youth learn from the pros.

Another fun idea is to have the older participants bring photos of themselves from high school. Pictures from earlier days don't have to be from school, but yearbooks and annuals would add to the atmosphere of prom.

Mixing the youth and the older generations at your church, a prom revisited allows the teens to appreciate the older members of your church. Even though older adults and youth seem miles apart, this event will help the youth see that these folks really weren't so different when they were teens—and that some still aren't that different.

CHAPTER 3
IDENTITY MARKERS

How do your youth celebrate who they are? This chapter provides ideas for marking the identity of the group as a whole and the identities of individual group members.

These ideas will help you create an environment that screams, "Youth!" and one that youth will want to be a part of. From physical surroundings to the manner of celebrating, this chapter includes ideas to create a group identity in which youth will be proud to claim membership.

Individual identities are just as important as the group identity. This chapter is full of ideas for celebrating milestones such as birthdays and academic and extracurricular achievements. Use these suggestions to affirm your youth and their accomplishments. Celebrating the

identities of individuals in the group allows the group to grow closer and enhances the whole group identity at the same time.

This chapter points out opportunities to help your youth mark their identity as a group of Christians. Help your teens discover who they are as children of God through church visits, prayers, and blessings to one another.

Having an identity affirms their uniqueness as a creation of God and allows them to express that creation. A group identity provides comfort, camaraderie, and assurance of belonging; it allows youth to feel part of a larger family. Use these identity markers to strengthen your group and give your) youth the encouragement they need.

IDENTITY MARKERS

STUDENT LEADERSHIP

As youth workers, we are in ministry with youth, not providing ministry as entertainment for them. Your youth may enjoy the programs and events you plan, but don't leave them out of making decisions. Including teens in youth group leadership ensures active participation. And as we all know, the more one is invested, the more he or she cares. Youth need to have ownership of their group, and student leadership provides a way for them to do so.

You can use several student leadership models, but a trusted "oldie but goody" is the officer and representative format. If your youth group is divided by junior high (or middle school) and high school, have each group elect its officers. This format helps establish ownership and identity in each group. If you have one large group encompassing all ages, then one set of officers is fine.

Officers include president, vice president, secretary, treasurer, chaplain, and historian. Depending on the size of your group, combine responsibilities or add other positions . to fit your needs. Representatives are exactly what their title sounds like: They represent each grade level, serving as sounding boards for their groups. Have one, two, or three representatives from each grade elected to maximize youth involvement.

The group should elect all officers and representatives, and youth interested in positions should be given the opportunity to tell the group why they would be right for the jobs. Use a secret ballot to vote and tally the results in private. Do not count votes out loud in front

of the group. This mistake can lead to hurt feelings and embarrassment for teens, resulting in the opposite of what you're trying to accomplish.

Make sure that officers and representatives stay involved in meetings, events, lessons, and scheduling for the youth group. Have monthly or quarterly meetings where youth plan the coming months. Just remember that being involved in leadership doesn't mean making all of the final decisions. As adult leader, you'll have to use your judgment to determine whether the youth leadership's ideas are feasible, appropriate, and realistic.

In addition to planning, have specific duties for each officer to perform at weekly meetings. The youth should make announcements, lead singing, recognize new people and visitors, lead games, celebrate those with birthdays, collect offerings, present devotions, and so forth. Do what fits your group best.

MEMBERSHIP CARDS

Some youth groups use membership cards to help reinforce group identity. Much like uniforms, membership cards serve as a unifier by connecting those who display them.

Membership cards can be as simple as a piece of paper with a student's name and the name of the youth group. Or they can be laminated cards with photos and contact information. Decide what is best for your group.

If you take photos of youth for their membership cards, use a digital or instant camera. Include other information such as student name, grade, and phone number. On the back of the card, have important phone numbers, including the church's number and the youth leader's home or cell phone number, so that in an emergency the youth can reach someone. Some youth groups are large enough to have student numbers and even bar codes on cards for registering attendance.

Involve the youth by having them design the membership cards. If your group or church has official colors, use them on the cards. Laminating the membership cards will greatly increase their life span.

YOUTH GROUP T-SHIRTS, HATS, BRACELETS, PINS, AND MORE

Who says you can't wear your pride on your sleeve? Group T-shirts and other apparel help your teens connect and identify with one another in a visual way. Bands, choirs, athletic teams, and businesses use uniforms to identify their groups as united and unique. The same principle applies to youth groups.

Wearing the same type of clothing facilitates a connection between persons. The sense of belonging and inclusion that comes with identical shirts explains the success of brand and slogan shirts sold at popular outfitters. Fans wear team colors to show unity and are connected through their support of the team. Create team colors in the form of a T-shirt for your youth group.

Increase the excitement of a group T-shirt by having a shirt-designing contest. Open the contest to everyone in youth group, and let the youth judge the submissions. After selecting a design, take orders and have the shirts made with that design on them. Be sure to order extras for those who didn't order shirts but change their minds when they see the rest of the group in their new gear.

Some groups have one shirt for the entire youth group. Other groups opt for a separate shirt for the junior high

or middle school group and the senior high group. Some large groups have different shirts for each grade level. Shirts that are available only to those in the group create a special sense of belonging and connection.

Besides helping teens look good and feel positive about belonging, group T-shirts make it easier to keep track of youth when traveling with a large group. Perfect for mission trips, youth rallies, or any outing to a heavily occupied setting, group T-shirts will make your teens stand out, making them a more visible witness and easier to keep track of.

Youth group T-shirts allow teens to feel they belong to the group and are an important part of the whole. With youth group T-shirts, hats, and so forth, your youth will wear a sense of pride and inclusion on their . . . well . . . sleeves. Check *www.cokesbury.com/specialtyimprints/* as a source for your group T-shirts.

NEWSLETTERS, CALENDARS, AND E-NEWSLETTERS

A youth newsletter and calendar are practical because they inform everyone of youth activities. But people often overlook a newsletter's ability to develop identity. The layout and presentation of a youth newsletter can express your group's uniqueness. You don't want a youth newsletter to look like *The Wall Street Journal*; if kids like that look and format, they probably already subscribe to it. Instead, give the youth group newsletter a look of its own.

To develop a newsletter with a look youth will like, have them design it. Who says it has to start on a right-hand page and open up to a two-page spread? And why do you have to print in black ink on white paper? You don't! Be creative and let the ideas flow.

Let the youth be the writers. Teens will more likely read something they hear from other youth in current lingo than from an adult. Youth don't

need a journalism degree to write about a coming event, but they may need some help in proofreading.

Have the group come up with a catchy name for their newsletter. The name can be closely related to the church newsletter, or it can be totally new.

If you're thinking there's no way your youth could put together a newsletter, remember that these kids know more about computers than we do. If some of your youth have an interest in journalism or graphic design, this project would give them the perfect opportunity to get involved.

A youth newsletter that is distinctly youth-oriented will develop identity for your group and provide a creative outlet for those seeking a challenge.

YOUTH GROUP DEVOTION BOOKS

Do you have trouble finding devotional books that keep your teens' interest? If so, consider getting the youth to write devotions themselves.

Recruit teens to write for a book of daily devotions to be handed out to the youth group. Give them a format such as Scripture passage, teaching, and prayer. Have the youth choose a topic for their devotions, or give them a pre-selected topic or Bible passage. Let the teens study the passage and develop their thoughts, then have them write a devotion based on God's message. They should also write an appropriate prayer to end their devotional message. Encourage them to present artwork, poetry, and photos for the book.

Have contests to design the cover and to name the devotional book. You might produce this book

once, continually, annually, or seasonally. Advent and Lent are two great seasons for a youth group devotional book. Let the youth help one another understand the meaning behind these seasons by relaying their feelings, thoughts, and experiences. If your group has monthly themes, use this devotion-writing to reinforce the youth group focus by coordinating the monthly theme with the devotional book theme.

As editor, change only grammatical and punctuation errors and elements that are significantly out of line. Don't rewrite a youth's entire devotion and make it something it was never meant to be.

You may decide to use this book to engage kids in daily study and prayer. Youth will likely commit to this activity, because they want to read what their friends say.

Youth group isn't the only possible audience for a devotion book. Make extra copies, and distribute them to other members of the church.

ENDING PRAYER AND BENEDICTION

To help establish identity in your group, have a standard ritual to end your meetings. Establish a tradition of praying together and sending one another off with a benediction.

A benediction is a blessing usually used at the closing of a gathering. It is the last spoken part of a meeting and leads participants in going forth into the world.

A common Scripture used as a traditional benediction is Numbers 6:24-26: "The LORD bless you and keep you; the LORD make his face to shine upon you, and be gracious unto you; the LORD lift up his countenance upon you, and give you peace." Aaron and his sons were to give this blessing to the Israelites.

Many affirming blessings from the Bible can be used as a benediction. But your benediction doesn't have to be from the Bible. Have the youth group write its own benediction and end every meeting by saying it aloud. Encourage the teens to honestly pray this blessing to other members of the group rather than treating it as a memorized formality to end a meeting.

To help youth learn the benediction, paint it on the wall. If painting is not allowed, print the blessing on paper and display it on the wall. Have the kids decorate the paper so that it looks fun.

YOUTH GROUP COVENANT

A covenant is more than an agreement or a pact. It's even more than a promise. A covenant is a commitment with God that is bound by God. Think about these important covenants God made:

• God's covenant with Noah to never again destroy the earth with water (Genesis 9:8-17)

• God's many covenants with Abraham (Genesis 12, 15, 17)

• God's covenant with the Israelites in the desert (Exodus 19–24)

• God's new covenant: Jesus Christ

When we covenant with one another, we are not just agreeing to try something; rather, we are saying to one another, "With God as our partner and with God's help, we promise to . . . ". By covenanting, we acknowledge that our commitment is founded and based in Christ.

Making a covenant with your youth group helps the teens establish group identity and become closer. A group covenant serves as the guiding agreement for expectations of youth group members.

Have a session with the entire youth group, and establish rules by which your group agrees to abide. These regulations can cover everything from the way the teens speak to one another to cell phone etiquette at meetings. They should address issues of respect and living together in Christian love. Whatever guidelines your group decides on, make sure your group understands the expectations of every member of the youth group.

When the covenant is complete, place it in a convenient location where it is visible to the youth. For dramatic flare, print the covenant on a large piece of paper that the youth can sign. Frame the covenant and hang it on the wall in the youth room. Or, if you're allowed to do so, paint the covenant on a wall and have the kids sign the wall.

First Church Youth Group Covenant

Because we are a community of growing disciples, we will love, respect, and nurture one another as brothers and sisters in Christ. We will not say hurtful things or have negative attitudes. We want to build one another up and speak the joy of living in relationship with God to everyone who comes here.

LETTERMAN JACKET PINS

Letterman jackets are as popular today as they were in the fifties, sixties, and seventies. Jackets have always been costly, but today's versions cost hundreds of dollars because of everything that comes with them: varsity letter, student's name, class year, school name, mascot, sport or sports played, musical group, art group, and so forth. This list doesn't touch on the pins, medals, bars, stars, and patches for extra achievement.

Whatever items come on a letterman jacket, teens get excited to wear one. Youth work hard to earn their jackets and take pride in their accomplishments. Now teens can be proud of their youth group involvement and add a special touch to their letterman jackets.

Create a pin or patch to award the youth when they earn their letterman jackets. The pin or patch should represent your youth group and the student's commitment to Christ. There is no right or wrong shape for the pin or patch, but it should represent your group. You can order cross-shaped patches in school colors to match jackets, or you can place a special pin on the students' jackets. If you choose pins, have your youth group design them or purchase basic, predesigned pins.

The youth in your group will appreciate the gift and take pride in telling others they are part of a community of Christian believers. These pins make a great evangelism tool too. When other teens see the pin or patch, they will ask about it and your youth can tell them why they have it and where they got it.

For those who don't letter in a sport or activity, award them a pin or patch based on their involvement and commitment to that activity. Another option is to give a pin or patch to everyone in the group so that no one feels left out.

BOOK COVERS AND BINDERS

Every fall, school books face the threat of being scratched, scraped, spilled on, bent, doodled on, and defaced in lots of ways. One way to protect books from damage is to put them under a bed and never open them. A more practical way to protect a book is with a book cover. It's not a bullet-proof vest, but it will guard a book against minor accidents and a wandering ink pen in the hands of a bored student. And that protection can save the student money when it comes time to turn in books.

To make book covers, provide paper with the youth group logo or a student's design on it. (If you don't have a logo for your church or youth group, use a cross.) Or talk with a printer about colorful designs that can be customized for use as book covers. Imagine all of your youth group members walking around campus with their custom-made book covers. A Christian symbol or Bible verse on the cover makes an excellent witness tool. It also reminds youth to whom they belong and that they are never alone.

If your budget doesn't support custom-printed book covers, make them from scratch by cutting brown paper bags, folding them, and taping them to fit each book. Have a book-cover-making party where the youth bring their books and paper bags. Another low-cost option is to use colored butcher paper from a large roll. If you want to get adventurous, try different types of materials, such as aluminum foil or burlap fabric. Give awards for the best decorated, most colorful, or most unique book cover.

PHOTO ALBUMS AND SCRAPBOOKS

Memories of events can be just as important as the event itself. Youth love to relive their experiences from youth group mission trips, camps, and other outings. To organize and store memory-jogging photos and souvenirs from those times, compile photo albums and scrapbooks.

Photo-album making can be as basic as putting pictures into an album. To add a personal touch everyone will enjoy twenty years down the road, write the names of the people pictured on the back of or below each photo, along with the event name and date. Labeling photos will help make memories last.

Scrapbooks are photo albums on steroids. Spice up youth group photos by making a scrapbook that covers each youth group trip, activity, or major event. Since memories are more than photos, include programs, tickets, maps, postcards, and any other remembrances from the trip. Scrapbooking requires more time and energy than compiling photo albums but results in a true treasure.

Because of the popularity of scrapbooking, someone in your church probably has a passion for it. Tap into that person's enthusiasm, and have him or her organize youth who are interested in creating scrapbooks.

With photo albums or scrapbooks, include written stories and memories from youth. This addition provides context for those who flip through the book of memories years later.

If "paper" memories aren't your thing, try video scrapbooking. Instead of putting photos and stories into a book, burn them onto a CD. This inexpensive method provides each youth with a copy of the photo album or scrapbook. If your church doesn't have a digital camera, use a scanner to download photos. Once you have electronic versions of the photos, e-mail them to youth or post them on the youth website for downloading.

WHO AM I?

This fun quiz helps youth group members learn more about one another. Discovering more about their peers will bring amazement to the youth.

Choose one youth from the group to be the mystery person, and interview him or her prior to your weekly meeting. Make sure nobody knows whom you interviewed. Have him or her fill out a questionnaire with these questions:

- Where were you born?
- How many brothers and sisters do you have?
- What's your favorite TV show?
- Do you have any pets?
- What do you want to be when you get older?
- What do you like to do in your free time?

Feel free to come up with additional questions that will help the youth get to know one another better. You can include this questionnaire in the youth newsletter as an article, post it as an independent flier on a bulletin board, hand it out at weekly meetings, or post it on your youth website.

After the youth returns the questionnaire to you, read the answers to the group by beginning each sentence this way: "I was born in . . . . I have . . . brothers and . . . sisters. My favorite TV show is . . . . I have . . . dogs and . . . cats. When I get older I want to be . . . . In my free time I like to . . . ." Then ask the group, "Who am I?" Have the youth guess the identity of the person.

Provide a prize for the first three people who correctly guess the identity of the mystery person. For example, the first three people to correctly guess the person's identity could win lunch with that person and the youth director at the restaurant of their choice (as long as the place offers an appropriate setting and reasonably priced meals). Give candy to those who guess correctly but aren't one of the first three. If you do the lunch as a prize, have a rule that a person cannot win lunch two consecutive times. This regulation will help spread out the winners.

This game gets kids asking questions about one another. In attempting to figure out who the mystery person is, the youth will engage in conversation and learn a little more about their fellow group members. Sometimes kids are amazed to find out their best friend is the answer.

After conducting one guessing session, post the answer and the winner. Youth will have fun competing to find out who the person is, and without realizing it they'll be getting to know one another better.

48   *Marking Milestones and Making Memories for Youth: Looking Back . . . Looking Forward*

RECOGNIZING GUESTS AND VISITORS

Does your group have a unique, unintimidating way of recognizing visitors and new people at youth meetings? New people can find it scary to stand up and introduce themselves in front of a group of people they don't know. Many times, new youth didn't really want to be there in the first place and have come because someone "forced" them to go. Making them stand up and talk in front of the group is one way to increase their apprehensions about going to youth group.

Instead of having new people introduce themselves, have a member of the youth group introduce them. Designate specific youth as "introducers," who have the responsibility of meeting new people during the few minutes before youth group starts then introducing them at the appropriate time. If the introducer doesn't recognize someone, he or she simply walks up to that person and greets him or her. Then the introducer finds out whether the person is new, a friend who came with someone else, or just someone who hasn't been at youth group for a long time. When the time comes for recognizing new people, the introducer stands in front of the group and introduces the new person.

You may want to give a small gift to all first-time visitors. Some groups use a candy bar, soda, or other snack food. Other groups use bookmarks with youth group information on it.

If the new youth are comfortable, take a picture of them and post it on a welcome board. Send a follow-up letter from the youth group to each new person no later than a week after his or her visit.

Having a non-threatening way of recognizing visitors and new people to your youth group will provide a more pleasant experience for everyone. New youth will feel welcomed without feeling pressured.

RECOGNIZING BIRTHDAYS

How does your group celebrate birthdays? While most adults try to forget they're getting older, youth live for these special days. As a youth group family, you should do something special to acknowledge each member's birthday. Here are some fun ideas:

- Create a birthday board with names and dates posted for everyone to see. Be creative and use different fonts, colors, shapes, and sizes. Cover a month at a time so that the board changes and stays fresh. The youth will know that the board changes and will rush to see their names and birth dates when their birthday month rolls around.

- Reserve a space in each youth newsletter or calendar to list names and dates. The kids will surely turn to this section each time they receive a newsletter.

- At weekly youth group meetings, recognize the youth who have had birthdays during the past week or those who have birthdays in the coming week. Develop a tradition of celebrating birthdays. Some groups call the birthday honorees to the front and sing to them, while others just have them stand up. Some groups sing "Happy Birthday" in the usual way, and others sing a different style (such as country, metal, Elvis-like, opera, and with a British accent).

- Have a special birthday prayer the group says for all group members celebrating birthdays. Invite the youth to write a prayer that thanks God, asks for blessings, and celebrates the gifts they have received. Use the prayer as part of your weekly birthday observation.

- As an alternative to weekly recognition, try having a monthly party. Celebrate birthdays for the whole month all at once. Choose one day and have a party with cake and ice cream for the whole group. Point out those who have a birthday that month and sing to them. Give each of those youth a card signed by the whole group.

Having a special way to recognize birthdays establishes identities in your group. This small and perhaps seemingly insignificant routine will start a tradition that youth anticipate and enjoy—it's fun for those having birthdays and for the rest of the group as it helps them celebrate.

CHURCH VISITS AND DISCUSSIONS

To help your group identify who they are as a group and as Christians, plan visits to other houses of worship. These outings will allow your youth to compare your church with other denominations or religions.

Set aside a couple of weeks or more, depending on the number of visits you want to make, and plan a lesson series that examines other denominations or religions. Begin the series with your church's beliefs and the basic beliefs of the Christian faith.

If you use this activity as a study of the differences between denominations, start with a quick history of the Christian church and the Reformation. Make sure the youth know that denominations are different groups within the whole of the Christian religion. Lutheran, Episcopal, United Methodist, Catholic, and Baptist are some examples of Christian denominations. Even though these denominations have differences, their basic faith is based on Jesus' life, death, and resurrection. Visiting several denominations gives your group a peek into different ways Christians worship, pray, and live out their faith.

If you use this activity as a comparative look at religions, tell the youth what makes Christianity unique, so that the they have a foundation from which to examine other religions. Visit synagogues and mosques, and invite rabbis and clerics to tell your group about their respective faiths.

Afterward, go out for ice cream and discuss what the youth found similar to or different from their church. Find out what made the teens uncomfortable and what they liked. What didn't they understand? What really stood out to them?

If your group has just visited a non-Christian house of worship, talk about how Christianity views this particular religion. Then discuss how we as Christians are to view other religions. How are they viewed by God? What does the Bible say about other religions?

Visiting other churches and places of worship gives kids the chance to discover and explore who they are as Christians. Most youth take an interest in others' beliefs and will appreciate this chance to learn with the group.

P.S. This activity ties in well with guest speakers. Ask a Catholic or Orthodox priest, Jewish rabbi, and Muslim cleric to be part of a panel discussion about the differences and similarities of each faith.

PALM SUNDAY HANDPRINTS

This activity does not involve a triumphant entry into Jerusalem, but it's a fun way to celebrate your youth group. Do you have a blank wall in the youth room that needs decorating? Well, here's your opportunity: Palm Sunday handprints, which are like fingerpainting but with the whole hand.

Use this activity to add a personal touch to youth room decorations. Have the teens paint their hands then press them against the wall. Each person gets to put one set of prints on the wall (one left hand and one right hand). Let youth be creative with how they paint their hands. for example, the hands don't have to be all one color. When the paint dries, have the youth sign their masterpieces.

This activity is also a "handy" way to remember graduating seniors. Some youth groups have a special senior wall or wall of fame where graduating seniors paint a lasting, parting message to those who will follow. If the youth room has a cinderblock wall, use the natural grooves as boundaries and give each senior a rectangle to decorate. You can limit decorations to handprints, autographs, and class years, or you can leave it up to each youth.

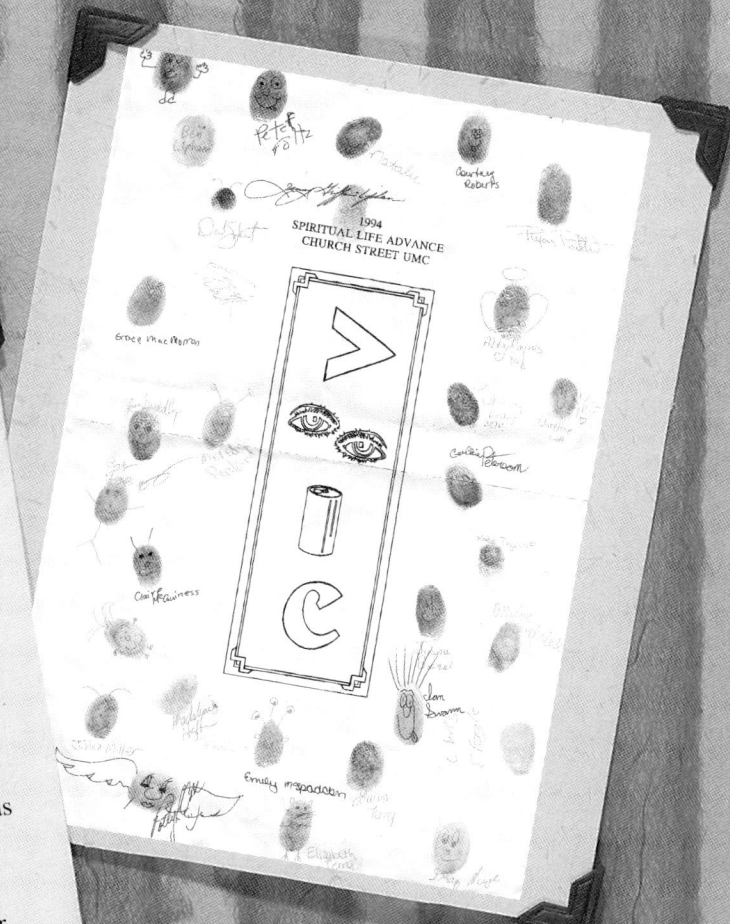

Some might paint their areas from edge to edge, and others might simply sign their names.

If your group can't paint on the wall, provide tiles to each youth. Again, the youth can decorate their tiles and hang them on the wall in a non-permanent manner.

Always popular, the handprint castings outside Planet Hollywood restaurants and Grauman's Chinese Theatre in Hollywood attracts people to place their hands in the handprints of the stars and see how they measure up. Celebrating the star quality of everyone in your group with Palm Sunday handprints allows the kids to leave a bit of themselves with the group. The handprints can also be developed into a custom your youth look forward to every year.

GOLD RECORDS

This identity builder is based on an idea in a participants' booklet from a Youth Specialties leader-training seminar. Most youth have never owned a record player; they use CD players instead. But most youth are familiar with the phrase *album of the year* and know that albums go gold and platinum. (Having a record go gold or platinum refers to the number of album units sold. When an artist has an album go gold, platinum, double platinum, and so on, the record company presents the artist with a framed, platinum-colored album and plaque.)

You can use the idea to create special recognition for individuals. Print a label

with the students' name and your affirmations in place of the artist name and song titles. Frame and present the album to your honoree.

You can also create this memory maker for the whole group. When making the gold or platinum records, use the youth group name as the record company and the class year as the record title. For song titles use the names of the students in that class.

Frame the record and hang it in the youth room as a tribute to seniors. If you repeat this display each year, the youth will look forward to their record-setting debut. When youth come back from college, they can see their names still on the wall.

In addition to making the class record, give each member of the class a smaller version of the wall-mounted tribute using CDs. If you have the technology, burn the CD with photos of class members and of youth group activities from the past year.

VIDEO YEARBOOKS

You're familiar with the concept of a yearbook: a review of the past year comprised of photos, stories, and remembrances. Well, why not have a youth group yearbook? To make it more interesting to youth, create a video or digital yearbook.

This activity will require some technological knowledge, and some groups might find the cost of equipment prohibitive. But let's face it: Youth are into anything technologically advanced. They burn CDs, create movies, and spend lots of time online. Take advantage of their technological interests and skills, and have the kids help create a video yearbook for your group.

DVDs of youth group events will make great yearbooks. Take videos from past events and edit a compilation that leads viewers on a tour of the past year. Interview the youth about the past year and the ups and downs they been through. Include a rundown of popular songs, movies, and important world events, so that the kids have a reminder of what they lived through.

If your budget doesn't allow for making a DVD, burn a picture onto a CD to give to students. Take still pictures from the past year, and put them on a CD for youth to keep. In addition to photos, include lists of popular songs, movies, and important events. Take digital photos of everyone in the group, arrange them by grade level, and place them on the CD as they would appear in a regular yearbook.

Another low-cost option is to create disks immediately following a youth group trip or event. By putting photos on the disk, you'll create a great memoir of the activity.

These yearbooks make great end-of-the-year gifts, and the youth will like having memories they can watch on TV or pop into the computer.

CHAPTER 4
TEARJERKERS

Are you looking for ideas that tug at the heart, push beyond the superficial, and help youth approach one another and God with sincere love? If so, this chapter is for you. These activities challenge youth to examine themselves, care for one another, and join together in Christian community.

When conducting these activities, you give youth the tools to reflect on their faith journeys, so that you may guide them in discussions on how to live a God-centered life. The following pages include ideas for enhancing worship by creating a more intimate experience through presentation, setting, drama, music, and prayer. Explore the options for worship in nature amidst God's creation.

Use these ideas to affirm the youth as children of God who have infinite hope through Jesus Christ. Empower them to care for one another through the affirmation ideas later in the chapter. God calls us to participate in a community based in love, a family of brothers and sisters. Live out that love through the affirming acts of caring and through celebrating the diverse and unique parts of your youth group.

These ideas might not cause waterfalls of tears, but that effect is not the goal—you want to deepen their relationships with God and leave a lasting impression they will carry with them for years and perhaps the rest of their lives.

DRAMAS

If you want an effective tool for communicating a message to youth, try drama. The majority of what we learn comes from what we see. And teens take in visual information much faster than adults, as evidenced by TV, movies, and video games. Therefore, taking a message and presenting it in a visual way will interest youth and communicate to them in a powerful way. When youth are open to hearing the message, it can make a difference in youths' lives that will last a lifetime.

Use drama as a discussion starter for topics that are difficult to explain or talk about. One such drama called *Maria* illustrates the idea that once we turn our lives over to God, we become new creatures in Christ. *Maria* is a monologue that revolves around a ceramic mask that represents Maria. A friend tells the story of how Maria, a beautiful young woman who enjoys life, starts to change. Maria struggles with fitting in at school, self-image, and living up to others' expectations. Eventually, Maria turns from her friends, parents, and God, becoming depressed in her burdensome existence. Finally, one night Maria gives control of her life to God and discovers that all of the darkness has been cleared away. Maria sees in herself the person God sees and becomes the new creation promised in 2 Corinthians 5:16-17.

While delivering the monologue, Maria's friend pours different colored paint over the white, ceramic mask that represents Maria. The friend drizzles bright colors down the face, creating a rainbow of colors when describing Maria's positive attributes. When life begins to get the best of Maria, the friend pours dull, drab colors onto the mask.

At the same time, the lights are gradually dimmed to darken the atmosphere as the world consumes Maria. At the point when Maria is at the end of her rope, the final light goes out and a crash is heard as the mask is broken with a mallet or hammer. After a moment of silence, in the dark, read 2 Corinthians 5:17. ("So if anyone is in Christ, there is a new creation: everything old has passed away; see, everything has become new!") While the stage is still in darkness, a new, fully decorated, festive Maria is placed on the table. When the lights are turned on, the friend introduces the transformed Maria to the group and invites others to change their lives and surrender control to God.

This play is just one example of how powerfully drama can reach and touch youth. To involve the youth more, have them write dramas to be used with lessons. Dramas can provide some of the best memory makers your group will ever encounter. This one has stuck with me since I was in youth group.

YOUTH BAND OR CHOIR

Whether your church has an established youth band or choir or is just starting one, this aspect of youth ministry provides many opportunities to make memories. Some of the greatest memories are created on youth choir tours. It doesn't seem to matter where a choir tours; the journey leaves an indelible mark on youth and on adults.

Where you tour will be determined mainly by your budget. Remember that youth will have as memorable a trip traveling around your region in the church van as they would flying to another state. To have a successful trip, visit churches of different sizes. Out-of-the-way churches with small congregations are often the most welcoming and hospitable. Arrange to share a meal with congregations for whom the choir performs. To save money and make the trip more fun, stay with church families instead of at hotels. Plan an outing to an amusement park, swimming pool, or other local attraction as a fun day.

To include more youth, incorporate a drama into the tour. This aspect can add to your performance and your witness.

To provide memoirs the teens can take with them—literally—give out youth choir or youth band CDs or DVDs. If your choir goes on tour, have CDs and DVDs of the performance for sale. (Be sure you obtain permission for any copyrighted material your group performs.) Soundtracks and videos can be ordered at the performance then burned and shipped later. Or record a dress rehearsal before heading out on tour and have copies available at each stop. Even if you're not heading out on tour, have CDs and DVDs for sale at your church. Record concerts that highlight Christmas, Easter, or other seasonal music; then sell the CDs as a fundraiser.

Here are some more uses for CDs and DVDs:
• If your church has a video ministry, use the youth choir or band to create the soundtrack for videos.
• Make music videos to be shown at youth group.
• Play CDs made by the youth choir or band as the kids arrive at youth group meetings.

These options will create lasting memories in which youth will take pride because they created them.

NAILING SINS TO THE CROSS

Youth have been told that Jesus died on the cross to take away their sins, but do they know what that act means? They might have an abstract concept about a guy two thousand years ago who died on a cross and came back to life so that today our transgressions can be removed. Nailing their sins to the cross provides youth with a more concrete, tangible example of Jesus' sacrifice and God's redeeming grace.

This overnight activity works best at a retreat or camp, where youth are able to take a serious look at themselves and their faith. Beforehand, bring the cross, nails, and hammers. During the activity, challenge the youth to be honest with themselves and with God. Give them a piece of paper and a writing utensil, and have write down the answers to the following questions:

- Are you living the way God wants you to live? If not, what is in the way?
- What is keeping you from being the person God wants you to be?

Assure the youth that these answers are between them and God and that nobody will read or disclose what is on the sheets. (They need not write their names on the sheets.) Tell the youth that these stumbling blocks are the sins for which Jesus died—the sins God promises to remove through Jesus' redeeming sacrifice on the cross. Read aloud 1 John 2:1b-2: "But if anyone does sin, we have an advocate with the Father, Jesus Christ the righteous, and he is the atoning sacrifice for our sins, and not for ours only but also for the sins of the whole world."

After the youth are finished writing their sins on the sheets of paper, guide them to a cross lying on the ground in front of the group. Invite the youth to approach the cross, take a hammer, and nail their folded papers to the cross. As youth nail their sins to the cross, they should pray for God's grace in removing those stains from their lives. Have them pray for strength and courage to live without those sins. You can also have the youth pray for others as they nail their papers to the cross.

After all of the teens have nailed their sins to the cross, offer a prayer for the entire group and retire in silence for the night. While the youth are asleep, quietly remove their papers without reading any of them. Leave the nails sticking out of the cross. Take the papers and burn or shred them so that no one can ever read them.

You can elect to leave the cross with just the nails sticking out and the sins gone, or you might decorate the cross with flowers and different colored decorations. Leave the cross in the same place it was when the youth last saw it. The following morning, youth will notice the cross and see that their sins have been removed, their slates cleared, and their sins forgiven.

If you want flare, use flash paper for the kids to write sins on. Flash paper burns almost instantly without leaving ash and can be purchased at a magic supplies store. In front of the group, read a Bible passage while removing the folded pieces of paper from the cross. (Romans 3:23, Romans 5:6-9, Ephesians 2:1-10, 1 Peter 2:24, and 1 John 1:9 are good verses to use.)

Place the papers in a coffee can until the cross is bare of papers. Set the can on the ground, then light a match and toss it into the can. The paper will flame up (watch your eyebrows) and burn the papers in a matter of seconds. Then let kids see that their sins are gone. Mention that the cross has done something to the paper, so that the youth focus on the power of the cross instead of the power of the flash paper.

CANDLE LIGHTING

Use candles to enhance your worship space. A lone flame flickering in the dark has immense power. Have the youth stand in a circle around the candle and focus on the hypnotic rhythms of the flame as they give praise to the Holy Spirit. Create more impact by filling the worship space with dozens of candles of different shapes, colors, and sizes. The overpowering glow given off by dozens of candles is inspiring as the light shines in every direction.

While worshiping among the glow, ask God to make each individual member of your group shine as a light in the world. Pray that your group would glow with love, power, and grace, inspiring others to illuminate the world with the same infectious glow that radiates from the surrounding candles.

COMMUNION

Celebrating Holy Communion together is another vital aspect of Christian worship. Be creative in sharing this renewing meal as a group. While the power of Communion should be reason enough to be interested, let's face it: Youth aren't big on liturgical script. So rather than having the same Communion that occurs during the church service, mix things up in a way that will make the youth will embrace the Lord's Supper.

Changing the look and feel of Communion brings youth closer together in worship. Try changing the type of bread used for the service. Pita, wheat, white, sourdough, multi-grain, unleavened, and cinnamon raisin bread, as well as dinner rolls, pancakes, and bagels, can be used to symbolize the Body broken.

Try a different type of juice, and serve Communion in a way that is different from what youth are used to, such as intinction, common cup, sitting, standing, kneeling. Have the youth serve one another instead of just being served. By actively participating in Communion instead of passively watching and waiting, the teens will have a richer experience. For a great Communion idea, check out Clown Communion on page 54.

CHANGE SETTING AND TIME

The church sanctuary is a wonderful place for worship services. But if you're looking for a change, try moving to a new setting. Inside, outside, upside down—it doesn't matter. Have worship in the youth room, the gathering hall, the church. (Check out Worship in Nature on page 55.) Changing the time you worship can also provide a fresh perspective. Worship late at night, first thing in the morning, or all night long.

Changing the setting or time breaks the routine of worship and will re-engage youth, so that they invest themselves more in praising God. And when they do so, your worship will be genuine, honest, and memorable.

A VARIETY OF PRAYER TECHNIQUES

Another vital aspect to worship is prayer. Again, involving youth will make prayer more meaningful to your group. Instead of praying for your group, involve the youth in the praying. Have them write prayers to be used in worship, and provide opportunities for them to pray. Keep the prayers fresh and dynamic by mixing up the way you pray. Youth will enjoy different ways of praying, and by using different methods you will maximize the potential connection with and impact on youth.

Here are some methods of praying:

- **Silent prayers:** Participants pray on their own in a quiet offering to God.
- **Hand-squeeze prayers:** Standing in a circle and holding hands, participants pray out loud one at a time then squeeze the hand of the persons next to them when they are finished. Prayer begins with one person and continues until the last person has had a turn. If an individual doesn't want to pray aloud, he or she simply squeezes the next person's hand and the prayer continues.
- **Popcorn prayers:** Participants randomly speak their prayers aloud. Prayers just pop up from around the group. It's OK if more than one person speaks at the

same time. Since God is delighted that we pray, I doubt God gets upset when people pray simultaneously. Besides, youth don't seem to have trouble talking at the same time as others during lessons and discussions.
- **For-one-another prayers:** The youth list their prayer requests to the group, then a member of the group agrees to pray for that specific person and their requests.
- **Breath prayers:** The group repeats a one- or two-line prayer with each inhale and exhale.
- **One-word prayers:** Youth lift up one word aloud instead of disclosing intimate details. They will likely say words such as *school, friends, sister, illness, drama class,* and *basketball*.
- **Singing prayers:** Participants offer music to God in worship and praise.
- **Meditative prayers:** The group focuses on a subject and meditates on it for an extended period of time.
- **Guided prayers:** The leader mentions a topic, then the group offers up prayers. At the appropriate time, the leader guides the group to the next topic.

Many ways of praying exist. Choose different methods to engage youth in a new way, and change prayer from a spectator event to a participatory dialogue with God.

DIFFERENT TYPES OF MUSIC

Most people are familiar with hymns, songs, and praise music. But music can also complement other aspects of worship. Playing soft music during prayer can provide inspiration, as can background music while Scripture is read aloud. (This technique is especially effective with the Psalms, which were originally sung anyway.) And music can help set the mood for dramas.

Music can be performed live, or it can be recorded and played through the speakers. But don't limit your use of music to published, professional pieces. If any youth in your group compose music, use their pieces as a further offering during worship. Celebrate the kids' musical gifts as you celebrate God in worship.

AFFIRMATIONS

BALLOON BONANZA

Send an affirming message to your teens by surprising them with a balloon bonanza. You can bestow these gifts at special occasions, for a pick-me-up, or to just let youth know they're appreciated. Deliver a bouquet of a dozen or two dozen helium balloons to a youth while at school. Drop off the special package in the office for the teens to pick up. The youth will wonder why they've been called to the office then will beam with joy as their friends ask why they have balloons.

If one of your teens' school doesn't allow deliveries, take the balloons to his or her house. Arrange with the parent or guardian to deliver the balloons while the youth is out of the house. The teen will be surprised to find a room full of balloons when he or she returns home. And the youth will feel loved and important by receiving this surprise gift.

SNAPSHOT

Most youth are probably familiar with digital cameras and may not have heard the expression *snapshot*. Used to describe pictures, snapshots provide quick looks at past events and stir memories of that event. A snapshot is a photograph of one moment in time, as opposed to a video that records a series of moments.

This affirmation can take place on the way home from a youth retreat, mission, camp, trip, or any long event. Following a significant youth group trip or event, teens have lots of memories and stories. Snapshot is the perfect way for those who attended the event or trip to share those memories with one another and affirm their experience together.

Here's how snapshot works: If a person wants to relay a story or memory, he or she says, "Snapshot" then a word or two that will cue everyone else in on that memory. Since this activity resembles a snapshot instead of a video, comments should be a single word or phrase instead of a long story. For example, if you ran out of gas in the church van and the

ONE-WORD AFFIRMATION CIRCLE

In an affirmation circle, youth take turns standing in the center of the circle, and one at a time members of the circle say something positive about the person in the center. With a large group, an affirmation circle can take a long time, so try doing a one-word affirmation circle. This activity is the same as a regular affirmation circle except that each person in the circle can say only one affirming word about the person in the middle. Examples of one-word affirmations include *friendly*, *talented*, *devoted*, *focused*, *giving*, *selfless*, and *loving*.

group had to walk in the rain to a gas station, a youth might say, "Snapshot: running out of gas" or "Snapshot: walking in the rain."

Most snapshots will be memories the whole group knows about because the kids will already have relayed stories to one another. But don't get caught up in hearing the rest of the mystery story; just move on to the next snapshot.

An inside joke works well as an affirmation of the trip or event within the group that participated, because everyone gets the joke. But if aired in front of the whole youth group, an inside joke becomes a divider by making others feel they are outside the group because they don't get it. They don't have the inside scoop and may feel disconnected. Only do snapshot with the group that went on the trip, attended camp together, and so forth.

SCREAMING BARNEYS

Named after the goofy and always well-intentioned deputy of Mayberry in *The Andy Griffith Show*, the Screaming Barneys was a group of five Christian friends, of which I was a part, who formed a covert affirmation team. Members of a college-age Bible study, we decided that part of our ministry would be to anonymously deliver affirming gifts to others in the Bible study group.

At random times, completely unannounced, we would make visits to those in need. We would anonymously leave a gift along with a "Screaming Barneys" business card. The recipients would find the affirmation on their door steps, on the windshield of their cars, on their desks at work, and at other unexpected places. The Screaming Barneys would visit those who were sick, leaving get-well wishes and snacks on their doorsteps. We would leave an envelope of gas money on the windshield of a group member's car when he or she was low on funds.

A covert affirmation group, such as Screaming Barneys, lets youth group members know they are special. You may want to ask the seniors in your youth group to be team participants. The underclassmen will enjoy the gift of receiving affirmations, and the seniors will enjoy the gift of serving by providing the affirmations.

Come up with a creative name for your covert group and print business cards with the name or logo. The anonymity makes these affirmations special, so the participants must never reveal they are part of the group. The teens will know that someone in the group is offering these kind gestures, but the activity is more fun if the receivers don't know who is responsible.

CLOTHES PIN CLIP

You're probably familiar with the wooden, spring-loaded clothes pins used to hold bags of potato chips closed or to clip wet clothes to the laundry line for drying. These inexpensive wooden clips have another use: bringing affirmation, laughs, joy, and a test of skills as youth are challenged to pass the affirmation to others.

Write messages on clothes pins. You can write compliments, Scripture references, loving doodles, or any uplifting words. Try to place the clothes pins onto the youths' clothes without them noticing. Once the kids start finding the clothes pins and reading the attached affirming messages, explain to them that they should pass the pins on to another person.

SNACK ATTACK MINISTRY

Using the same principles as in the Screaming Barneys, establish a Snack Attack Ministry (SAM). This affirmation provides a small snack (such as a candy bar or pack of gum) to youth unexpectedly. You can make SAM a personal outreach you do for the youth, or a group of youth can do SAM for the rest of the group.

Design and print business cards, including a logo and the letters *SAM*, to be left with each snack. Have a Bible verse on the card to reinforce the affirmation. John 15:17, which says, "This is my command: Love each other" (NIV), lets youth know they're loved. At opportune times, snack attack the youth by leaving the candy and calling card for them. Great times for a snack attack are after a hard day and before or after a sports event, concert, play, or any other extracurricular event. But there doesn't have to be a special reason to snack attack—you can do it just because you want to.

This affirmation is a small yet effective way to let youth know they are special and loved. And what speaks to youth as loudly as snacks?

CARE CARDS

When a significant event occurs in the life of one of the youth, send him or her a care card. For added personal touch, have the group members design and decorate a giant card made of posterboard. Have everyone in the youth group write a message and sign his or her name on the card. You may send care cards for birthdays, illnesses, and congratulations. Send care cards through the mail or drop them off in person and visit the recipient.

STICKY-NOTE SATURATION

Create a memory that will stick with the youth and let them know how special they are to you. You'll need a pack of adhesive notes and a pen or pencil. Write a blessing, affirming message, or Bible verse on each note, then stick it in a place where the recipient is sure to find it. Writing the same message on each piece of paper provides a repetitive affirmation youth love. Use a lot of notes so that the area is saturated.

This affirmation has a greater impact if it comes as a surprise. You can leave your name with a note, but you need not do so since the youth will know it's from you. (Who else would plaster adhesive notes all over the place?)

If you use Bible verses for the affirmation messages, either write out the verse or just write the Scripture reference. By listing only the reference, you present the youth with a mystery they can solve only by opening their Bibles. The wonder will last longer when they ponder what these notes could possibly mean. For a verse that will tug at the youths' hearts, try Philippians 1:3-4, which says, "I thank my God every time I remember you, constantly praying with joy in every one of my prayers for all of you." If you use a funny or random verse, such as the list of the dimensions for Noah's ark or Deuteronomy 29:11, you'll know whether the youth have looked up any of the verses because they'll ask you why you included that verse.

You can place the sticky notes almost anywhere. Put them in youths' rooms, on the doors to their rooms, on their lockers at school, on their cars, at their work places, or on their bikes or skateboards.

CARE NOTES

You may already send letters or cards to friends, but few groups have youth sending notes to their fellow group members. Prepare one envelope per youth with his or her name on the outside, or have the kids decorate their envelopes. Place all of the envelopes in your youth room, and provide paper and pens for the youth to write affirming notes to one another. Then have the teens fold the notes and place them in in the appropriate envelopes. Once a month, have the youth check their envelopes for messages.

Opening care notes are a great way to end a retreat, camp, or mission trip. Collect the messages during the event, and give the envelopes to the youth right before heading home. The teens will relive the event, remembering stories and memories as they read the affirmations from their peers.

CHAPTER 5
SERVICE AND OUTREACH

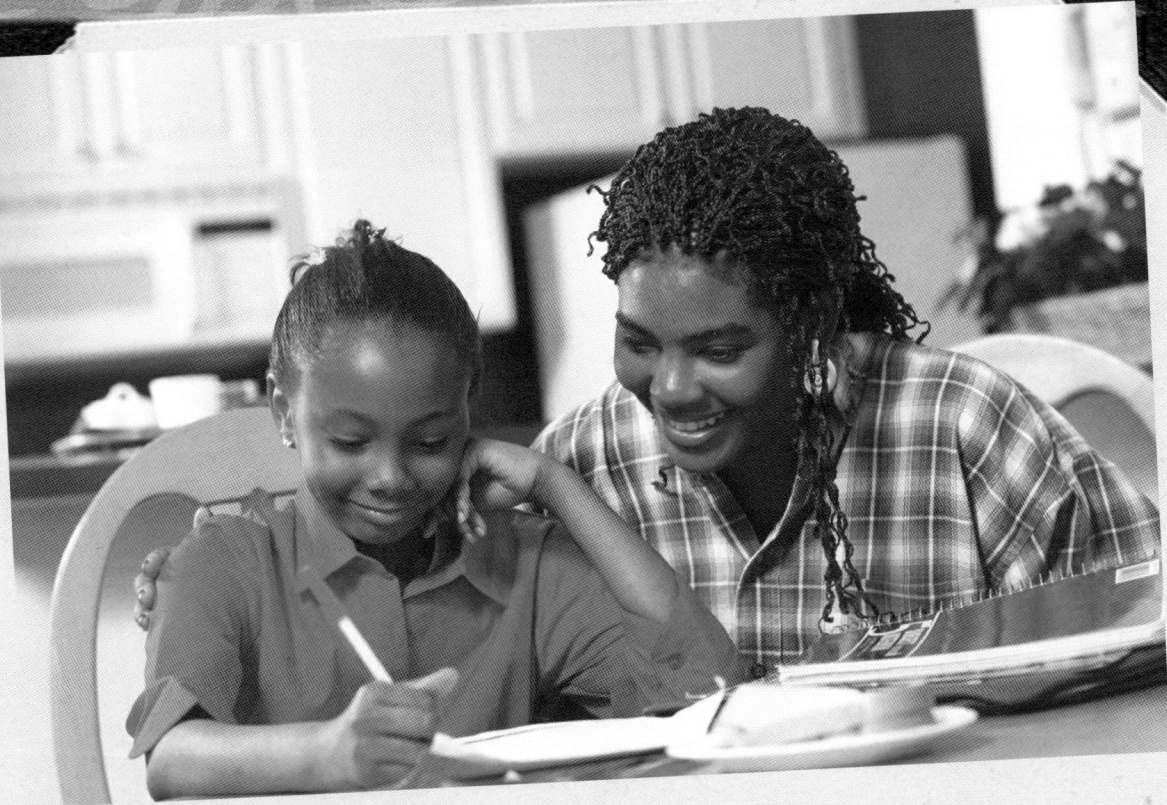

"The king will answer them, 'Truly I tell you, just as you did it to one of the least of these who are members of my family, you did to me.'"
(Matthew 25:40)

You don't have to stuff thirty people into a car or eat seventeen scoops of ice cream in one sitting to make memories. And although staying up for forty-eight hours straight and watching every *Star Wars* movie in order would be fun and memorable, that wouldn't necessarily contribute to God's work in the world.

This chapter provides ideas for your group to make memories while assisting others. Addressing issues from shelter and hunger to everyday needs such as school supplies, Service and Outreach has your group covered. You will find ideas for working face to face with people and projects that help people around the globe whom your youth will never meet. These activities will challenge your youth to sacrifice, live selflessly, and extend beyond their comfort zones in serving others.

Doing good deeds doesn't *make* you a Christian, and they don't get you into heaven. But as Christians we all are called to serve. And if we are truly living for God and not for ourselves, we will be doing good simply because God calls us to live that way. Use the ideas in this chapter to create memories while living out God's Word.

These memory makers may not seem as attractive or as exciting as skydiving, but the youth will find the memories far richer and valuable because they will know their actions have helped other people.

SERVICE AND OUTREACH

SOUPER BOWL SUNDAY

The football game, the time with friends, the commercials, and the food make Super Bowl Sunday memorable. On the day of the big game, Americans consume enough avocados to fill a football field from end to end, five feet deep. This day is also the single busiest day of the year for pizza deliveries. Consumers spend millions of dollars celebrating with decorations, drinks, and food. Meanwhile, many people go without sufficient food. Here's a way to make this day meaningful to youth while helping those in need: Have a Souper Bowl Sunday.

Souper Bowl Sunday is sponsored by the Souper Bowl of Caring, a group dedicated to hunger relief around the globe. Here's how Souper Bowl Sunday works: Youth groups collect food and financial donations at church on the Sunday morning of the Super Bowl game. Youth then decide which local area food bank or assistance organization to give the donations.

Teens count up the money and food donated and call the official Souper Bowl Sunday hotline 1-800-358-SOUP (7687) or visit *www.souperbowl.org* to report their totals. Souper Bowl of Caring compiles the reports from all of the youth groups from across the country and reports the grand total raised.

Advertise this event to the congregation a few weeks ahead of when the event will take place. On Souper Bowl Sunday morning, the youth will stand at the doors of the church, at the entrance to the sanctuary, in a designated area during coffee or fellowship hour, in the driveway of the church, or wherever works best and hold soup bowls for collecting donations. If you have a large church and soup bowls will be too small, hold pots and pans used for making soup.

The following week, tell the congregation how much your church has collected and how much the worldwide effort has raised. To find out the final numbers or obtain more information about Souper Bowl Sunday, visit *www.souperbowl.org*. For general information about hunger and poverty in the US and around the world, visit Bread for the World at *www.bread.org*.

SOUP AND SANDWICH VAN

Do you want to make a difference in a person's life? If so, turn the church van into a soup-and-sandwich delivery vehicle and hit the streets. Have the youth prepare soup and sandwiches to hand out to homeless and hungry people. They can keep the soup warm by storing it in a large, insulated drink cooler. These containers are normally used to keep drinks cold, but they also work well for keeping soup warm. Use a ladle to scoop the soup out; if the cooler has a spout, just push the button and fill a cup or bowl. (Don't use this button for pouring out chicken noodle soup, or else you'll be picking noodles out of the spout all evening.)

Pack pre-made sandwiches in small bags so that they're ready for the kids to hand out. Gather napkins and plastic spoons. Load everything up and head out to deliver soup and sandwiches.

Along with some adult volunteers, take your group to a local area known for its homeless. Park, open the side or back doors, and serve right out of the van. If it is easier to do so, bring a card table and set up a serving station. If homeless persons don't congregate in one area, drive around, pulling over when you see a homeless person, and serve him or her curbside from the street.

Feel free to expand this outreach to include handing out other basic items, such as blankets, toothpaste, toothbrushes, and the all-important but often overlooked underwear and socks.

VACATION BIBLE SCHOOL OR JAMBOREE FOR THE COMMUNITY

Most churches have a vacation Bible school for their own children, but what about those outside the church? We sometimes forget about those in close proximity to our home who need to be reached. A VBS or jamboree program for your community gives your youth a way to actively reach out and serve families in the community.

If a VBS isn't exactly what you're looking for or if it's too much "church" for those to whom you are reaching out, try a jamboree program. A jamboree is a hodgepodge of different activities in which children can participate; it includes everything from arts and crafts to games.

Have the youth plan and lead each area. The jamboree can be an unstructured time where participants make their way to different activities at their own pace. Or the youth can plan each area and activity and move the participants from one place to another at scheduled intervals. Almost any format can work, but the feasibility might depend on the number of participants.

Possible elements for a jamboree include coloring, making bead jewelry, outdoor games, singing, painting, lanyards, puzzles, story time, board games, puppet shows, and skits. In addition to such activities, include a devotion or other Christian message. The youth can use personal testimony, story time, puppet shows, sign language, and coloring to present Christian messages such as love, patience, and kindness. Remember that these participants are children, who have short . . . what was I going to say? . . . oh, that's right—attention spans. So keep each activity short. Lunch can be a big draw for children. They often appreciate sack lunches more than elaborate meals.

Invite the children's relatives to a final event. This time doesn't have to include a program the kids have been working on all week; it can be a big barbeque or celebration. A final event allows parents and guardians to visit the church and gives the youth a chance to invite families to attend the church.

If you feel that the community members would be too intimidated to attend a VBS or jamboree at your church, take the program into the neighborhood. Set up a tent or shade shelter in a front yard (with permission) and invite children to join the fun. This arrangement will provide a more comfortable atmosphere for those you are serving, and more of them might participate.

One of the best gifts you can give to the children in your community is a Bible. Hand out children's Bibles to those who attend the VBS or jamboree and let the children take them home. Holding a vacation Bible school or jamboree is a great idea for mission trips too.

CHRISTMAS IN JULY

You've probably heard about Christmas in July programs. But has your group ever participated in one? Christmas in July outreaches provide basic help and supplies for those who need food, clothing, toiletries, shelter, transportation, childcare, and debt-and-bill assistance.

During the Christmas season, many organizations and churches provide information about needy families for giving trees or angel trees, through which people can adopt these families and provide them with gifts. Christmas in July does the same service but during a different time of the year. And although the gifts can be similar to Christmas presents, they should include resources and supplies for basic, everyday survival.

Contact a local homeless shelter or service organization, and work with them to develop a list of specific needs; then determine the best way to divide the list. Provide a way for members of the youth group to "adopt" a family, or let the youth choose specific items from the list to contribute.

For a larger outreach, invite the whole church to join the youth in providing these much needed items. If you want this service project to feel like Christmas in July, have the youth, church members, or both groups bring all of their items on a particular day. Play Christmas music and drink hot cocoa while you organize and divide the supplies.

Giving youth the opportunity to make a difference in others' lives at a time other than Christmas prepares and trains them for a life of selfless service and helps them develop compassion for others.

BACK-TO-SCHOOL SUPPLIES DRIVE

The beginning of school was one of my wife's favorite times of the year, not because school was starting but because she got to go shopping for all of the cool, new school supplies: folders, pens, pencils, notebooks, rulers, compasses, protractors, and other "must have" supplies. Each fall, she still wanders through the aisles to check out the latest school supplies.

Some kids, however, never get to go shopping for new school supplies because their families cannot afford the items. Here's a way your youth group can change this situation: a back-to-school supplies drive. Contact local schools, shelters, food banks, or other organizations to determine when these items are needed and how to best distribute them.

Construct a list of basic back-to-school items, such as backpacks, paper, folders, pens, and pencils. (Local stores and schools often provide back-to-school lists in the late summer.) Include items for a variety of grade levels.

Have the youth collect the supplies and offer them to local schools, which can distribute them to students who are in need. Your teens can do their collecting by purchasing extra items when they shop for their own supplies, by seeking donations from local retailers, by doing a scavenger hunt for the items, or by inviting the whole church to bring items.

The group may never know who will receive the supplies and may never be thanked by the recipients. But that lack of contact doesn't matter, because your teens will know they have helped others. The youth will be content knowing that their contributions instilled pride and boosted the self-esteem of those who might otherwise be without. This activity is a small way to make a difference in someone's life.

PRE-MISSION-TRIP SCAVENGER HUNT

Going on a mission trip this coming spring break or summer? Instead of just raising money for more supplies, conduct a door-to-door scavenger hunt to acquire all or most of the supplies you will need. Most people don't have bricks, mortar, lumber, and cement lying around the house, so you'll have to buy some supplies. But you'll be surprised at how many supplies people do offer.

Before the scavenger hunt, create a list of items you need for your mission trip. Include everything from toiletries, paper products, and non-perishable food items to tools, paint, and hardware supplies (such as screws and nails). If you will be providing a vacation Bible school or children's program on your mission trip, include items such as crayons, Bibles, arts and crafts supplies, snacks, and costumes. On your list indicate the quantity of each item you need. Gather the whole youth group or divide it into teams, and have the youth go on a scavenger hunt to find as many of the needed items as possible.

Doing a pre-mission trip scavenger hunt not only acquires supplies and saves money; it also gets kids out and into the community to tell others about what they're doing. Youth have to explain their mission trips to those living in the homes they visit when asking for donations. When youth gather supplies as if they were playing a game, people are more willing to help. Often people can't give large cash or equipment donations to mission trips and projects, and with this scavenger hunt they don't have to. With one or two small items from each house, your group will soon have the supplies it needs.

Another option is to publish the list and challenge church members to bring items to church the following Sunday. This challenge provides a way for those who can't go on the trip to become involved in it. And some church members might be glad to have an excuse to clean out their sheds or workshops.

FOOD-BANK DRIVE AT A LOCAL STORE

A recent trend in service and outreach projects is to hold a food-bank drive at a grocery store. Arrange with a store in your area to spend a weekend (or longer) soliciting food donations for a local food bank or other charity. Group members can work in shifts at a station near the store entrance. Use signs, posters, and fliers to publicize your project as the group greets customers. Have your youth encourage the shoppers to purchase additional items and to donate them on their way out of the store.

Decide ahead of time whether to accept both food and cash donations. If you go with this option, donate the cash to the food bank, so that it may purchase perishable items such as milk and meat. The group can invite shoppers to purchase any non-perishable items they want or to help fulfill a list.

To develop a list, ask your local food bank what its greatest or most common needs are. Include the list on a flier to be handed out to shoppers on their way into the store. To highlight the needed items, go inside the store and place brightly colored, index-card-size signs that read, "Food Bank Need" next to the price tags of the selected products.

Another option is to pre-assemble "complete meal" grocery bags. Each bag should contain food for one complete meal: a main dish, a couple of side dishes, a bread product, and a dessert. Advertise the bags as complete meals for the needy.

If you want to let customers take a more active role in selecting items, hand out grocery bags with a list of eligible items stapled to the outside. From this list, shoppers can choose one item in each category (main dish, sides, bread, and dessert) and build a complete meal. Customers purchase the bag with their other groceries then drop it off on their way out of the store.

One last option for gathering food items is to challenge shoppers to match an item. This way, customers purchase two of an item instead of just one. One goes home with them, and one goes to the food bank. Stores often hold "buy one, get one half off" sales on select items. During these sales, this food-drive option provides a great deal for everyone: The store gets increased business, the customer gets a discount on helping others, and your youth receive more items for the food bank.

For information about hunger and poverty, visit Bread for the World at *www.bread.org*.

FIFTH-SUNDAY SERVICE PROJECTS

Fifth-Sunday service projects are exactly what they sound like—service projects that occur on every fifth Sunday. Instead of having regular youth group on those Sundays, have a service project. Use these fifth Sundays to practice what you've talked about during the past month.

Or conduct a service project on the last Sunday of each month. This way, you can work the service project into a monthly theme for your group. Lessons and discussions for the month revolve around a theme, and the service project on the final Sunday focuses on that idea. For example, a monthly theme on the environment might culminate into a service project where youth plant trees or pick up litter from a section of a road; a theme focusing on homelessness might wrap up with a service project at a homeless shelter.

Use fifth-Sunday or final-Sunday service projects to reinforce the lessons taught at youth group. Not only will they emphasize the message—they will also expose youth to several areas of need. Christ calls us to action, not just to awareness. Help the youth become aware, then equip them for service through these monthly projects.

CHRISTMAS-GIFT SURRENDER

Jesus said, "It is more blessed to give than to receive" (Acts 20:35b). At this comment, most kids, such as Arnold Drummond from *Different Strokes* would say, "What you talkin' 'bout, Willis?" We've all heard that giving is more important than receiving. We all know it's more difficult to give than it is to receive, but we also know God would want us to do so. So why don't we give more often?

Never is the divide between the poor and the wealthy more prevalent than at Christmas. A season of joy and celebration has turned into a commercial bonanza for businesses and a consumer's paradise for those with money. We delight in buying gifts for others almost as much as we enjoy receiving presents. Youth are told that giving is more important and more necessary than receiving, but the behavior we model contradicts our words. Youth learn from our behavior, comparing the gifts they receive with one anothers' gifts, writing extensive wish lists, and begging for the latest and greatest items. This conflicting message leaves youth confused. This Christmas, set the record straight and challenge youth to sacrifice for the benefit of others with a Christmas-Gift Surrender.

Christmas-Gift Surrender will create lasting memories, if not for the sacrifice and good it brings to others, surely for the uproar it will cause with some parents. (Don't youth usually delight in causing their parents stress?) Have each youth choose one of his or her favorite gifts he or she received for Christmas and give it to someone else. The youth might surrender their gifts to a shelter, charity, or other service organization. If you want to challenge youth even more, have them forgo all of their gifts and pass them on to the less fortunate.

If a Christmas-Gift Surrender is too "controversial" for your group and you hear too many moans and groans, make a gift wish-list for donations. Challenge the youth to send out letters to relatives asking that they make a donation to a charity instead of sending gifts. The relatives can choose which charity to donate to, or youth can list a local charity where donations should be sent. The teens can also ask a charity in advance what specific items it needs and then send the list in their letters. Surrendering a Christmas gift, or all of their gifts, is a tangible way for youth to sacrifice and live out God's call to put others first.

SHORT-TERM MISSION TRIPS

In his parting words before his ascension, Jesus said to his disciples,

Go ...and make disciples of all nations, baptizing them in the name of the Father and of the Son and of the Holy Spirit, and teaching them to obey everything that I have commanded you. And remember, I am with you always, to the end of the age.

(Matthew 28:19-20)

This call to serve is known as the Great Commission and is one of the main passages of the scriptural foundation for missions.

People sometimes differ on what a mission trip should be. Some feel it should consist of only construction and repair help, and others feel it should involve only evangelism and preaching. In my experience, a mix of both provides for the richest experience. Besides, if we are living our faith as we should, our actions will preach an evangelizing message while we work and play.

There is no right or wrong place to go for a short-term mission; domestic trips are as legitimate and worthwhile as international trips. So don't let destination be the focus of your trip but rather the connection with those you are serving. Many times in the Bible, God calls us to love one another, and in Matthew 19:19b God says that we should love our neighbors as ourselves. That principle applies no matter where you're physically located. The hard part is that your hometown isn't nearly as exciting or exotic as a small island off the coast of South America or a village in central Africa. Youth love adventure. What they don't know is that adventure is closer than they think.

Planning a mission trip can sometimes pose the biggest challenge of the trip. If you're new to these trips, feel you don't have the time, or just want a break from planning every little detail, try working through one of the many Christian service organizations that organize and sponsor youth mission trips. Here are a few established programs to get you started:

- Group Workcamps, www.groupworkcamps.org
- Sierra Service Project, www.sierraserviceproject.org
- Youth With A Mission (YWAM), www.ywam.org

Also, check out short-term mission opportunities within your church denomination.

An essential element to any mission trip is the right group attitude; humility, service, and openness to learning from those you are going to help. Conversely, an attitude of "we're going to go fix them—those other people" will result in an empty trip full of superficial memories of work. The wrong approach can cause a youth group to miss the very reason for missions.

As with other ideas in this book, having the youth involved in the planning and organizing will allow them to make the trip their own. With greater investment comes greater care and commitment. Bring your youth mission team together as a group in the months before your trip. Train together, play together, learn together, pray together, and then go together!

SIDEWALK CHALK MINISTRY

A package of chalk can bring lots of excitement to youth and children. There's something about the limitless possibilities of a blank canvas of concrete and asphalt. Changing it into a colorful, creative world instills a sense of belonging and ownership.

Take chalk into your community, and invite younger children to join in drawing and decorating sidewalks. Take plenty of extra packs of chalk so that your youth group can give one to each person they encounter. Encourage the participants to use the creativity God gave them to make the world a better place.

To minister to others, leave affirming, loving messages for others who will pass by after the group is gone. If you want to get people's attention, have the youth decorate the church sidewalks and parking lot on the evening before or morning of the worship service. The witness that people see as they arrive will leave a mark on them.

Your group can use this activity to bring new people through your church's doors. Adorn the sidewalks around your church with messages of greetings and invitations to join in worship or in youth group. After drawing arrows on the ground that guide people to the church, have the youth stand at the church doors to welcome people as they enter.

Use sidewalk chalk ministry to kick up your church's VBS, fall Sunday school program, communitywide Easter egg hunt, fall festival, or any other church activity. Chalk can also help advertise a communitywide VBS or jamboree the youth are sponsoring.

Sidewalk chalk is a fun, inexpensive way to reach out to others. It requires a minimal amount of supplies, and once people have chalk in their hands they're engaged. So break out the chalk and let the fun begin!

SPONSOR A CHILD

You've probably seen commercials about adopting a child for only a dollar a day. If you're typical, you probably didn't give much thought to the opportunity that was right in front of you. To act on this idea and help your youth make memories, organize the teens to sponsor a child.

Most of these programs involve a monthly payment that provides food, clothing, schooling, and medicine for a month. Sponsors receive a photo and biography of their child and have the opportunity to correspond through letters.

Sponsoring a child through these organizations should involve more than writing a check every month. The youth should take this endeavor seriously and fully invest themselves in it. To get the teens more involved, place the child's photo and biography on the youth room bulletin board and include information about the child you're sponsoring in your youth and church newsletters. On a regular basis, have your whole group write and sign letters to the child, and ask the youth to provide photos to send to him or her. You might even visit your child some day. Some organizations now allow sponsors to visit their children in person, and groups plan mission trips to the countries where there children live.

To raise money for the child, you might decide to take a weekly offering, do a special fundraiser, or give a percentage of all of your fundraising efforts to this cause. You may choose to sponsor one child as a group. Or, if you have a larger group, you might sponsor multiple children. If your youth program has a small-group ministry, have each small group sponsor a child.

Here are some organizations that specialize in child sponsorship:

- World Vision, www.worldvision.org
- Compassion™ International, www.compassion.net
- Christian Children's Fund, www.christianchildrensfund.com

DISASTER RELIEF

It seems that every day news agencies report some sort of disaster. Earthquakes, floods, hurricanes, fires, oil spills, tornadoes, and other disasters frequently strike without warning, causing tremendous losses. During extreme times like these, answering the call for help will make memories as your group comes together and focuses on the mission.

Lending physical assistance is most feasible when the disaster is close to you. Your group can help by cleaning up, serving meals, opening your doors for shelter, providing support services, and rebuilding. Don't underestimate the relief your youth can provide through seemingly mundane tasks. Filling sand bags, shoveling mud, picking up debris, and providing a hearty meal can make a huge difference in people's lives. Many ministries owe their beginnings to a group of people who volunteered to help with disaster relief.

If the disaster occurs in a different part of the world, helping in person can be difficult. Several organizations make it possible to help in other ways. One such organization is The United Methodist Committee on Relief. UMCOR responds to needs worldwide and, thanks to its giant warehouse, often provides assistance in the beginning hours after a crisis. UMCOR kits give youth one way to participate in relief efforts from right where they live anytime of the year. Specific, predetermined items make up each kit (UMCOR provides a supply list.) People collect items, assemble packages, and ship the kits to UMCOR. This organization then sends the kits to the region enduring the crisis.

Some examples of UMCOR Kits are flood kits, health kits, sewing kits, school kits, layette kits, and bedding packs. Flood kits include buckets, rags, scouring pads, scrub brushes, bleach, gloves, and other items needed to clean up after flooding. Health kits contain basic necessities such as washcloths, soap, toothpaste, and toothbrushes to help people stay disease-free and comfortable.

From disaster relief to refugee camps, kits are sent whenever and wherever in the world a need exists. These kits will provide everyday items that some people haven't had for weeks or months. And since The United Methodist Church funds UMCOR's overhead through church contributions, it uses one hundred percent of all donations to UMCOR for relief efforts.

Many similar organizations provide opportunities for your youth group to help relief efforts around the world. Here are just a few organizations to check out:

- UMCOR, *www.gbgm-umc.org/umcor/kits.cfm*
- World Vision, *www.worldvision.org*
- AmeriCares® at *www.americares.org*
- World Concern, *www.worldconcern.org*

ADOPT A FAMILY

Like sponsoring a child, Adopt a Family is an outreach where youth help make a family's life better. Contact local agencies to see if they have an Adopt a Family program. You can organize this outreach in various ways. Some people raise monthly dollar amounts that will provide for the family, and others have specific lists of needs from the family. Decide whether to give financial support or to supply specific items a family requests. Either way, the youths' personal involvement will make for a meaningful experience.

Be creative in raising funds or gathering supplies. Scavenger hunts, special fundraisers, and "bring an item a week" are fun ideas for involving youth. You might encourage the youth to donate a percentage of their babysitting and lawn-mowing money to your family. Or you could have them surrender their birthday and Christmas gifts for the family. (See Christmas-Gift Surrender on page 70.) This option works especially well if your group does extra service projects for Christmas.

NURSING HOME OUTREACH

Are you looking for a local outreach and service project? This one will allow the youth to use their gifts and talents while providing much needed services to older adults in your community. Arrange with a local nursing home or adult care facility to bring your teens over for a time of personal interaction with residents.

The youth should prepare several different activities to conduct at the nursing home. (Remember whom you're serving— sardines might be fun, but it's probably not an appropriate activity for nursing home residents.) Since some youth are intimidated by nursing homes and older adults, remind the youth that some of the nursing home residents do not have friends or family to visit them—most just want to talk and will be thrilled to have young people visit. Tell the teens to be patient, smile (especially if they hear the same story fifteen times), and speak slowly and a bit more loudly when talking with nursing home residents. Here are a couple of activities to try:

- **Story-Time Readings:** Gather the residents, and have the kids read a story aloud to them. Before they start reading, ask the youth to use different voices and inflections to convey separate characters and emotions. The readers don't need to be melodramatic, but they should make the story interesting by adding a dynamic touch. Props also make story time come alive. Beforehand, have the youth practice reading slowly, loudly, and clearly. If time allows and if the nursing home has a microphone, have the kids practice speaking into this device beforehand.

- **Reading the Bible:** As with Story-Time Readings, have the youth read the Bible to the residents. Many older adults have had to give up reading because of degenerating eyesight. Having someone read to those who can no longer enjoy reading on their own will bring them joy. Many nursing home residents were active in their churches and miss Christian companionship, Bible studies, and just reading Scripture. The youth do not have to read to older adults in a group setting; they can also read to them one on one. (This activity has the added benefit of youth reading the Bible.)

- **Worship Services:** Many older adults can no longer drive, and seldom, if ever, make it to church. If nursing homes don't offer worship services, residents don't get a chance to worship. So bring the worship service to them, planning a time of singing, Scripture, and a message. If the nursing home has a chaplain who offers worship services, see if your group can assist him or her with the service—they're always looking for help.

- **Sing-a-longs:** Put together a series of easy-to-sing songs for the residents. Have accompaniment for the songs, and let the youth lead singing. The songs should be a fun mixture of tunes from over the years, since the older adults probably won't know the latest hits. The group should not perform a concert for the residents but give them a chance to join in; the sing-a-long is for them, not for the youth.

Reaching out to older adults provides youth a way to serve those who are often forgotten. Using their gifts and talents, youth do activities they enjoy while meeting the needs of others. A nursing-home outreach doesn't have to be a one-time event; make it a regular part of your youth group schedule.

CHAPTER 6
HOLIDAYS AND ANNUAL OCCASIONS

Every year, my high school youth group would have a pancake breakfast following the Easter sunrise service. The youth would lead the service then dash to the kitchen to flip pancakes. This holiday event still brings back memories. Certain annual occasions, such as this one, are natural memory makers. Some might be used only once, and others will evolve into annual traditions that become part of the fiber of your group.

This chapter includes ideas for holidays such as New Year's Eve, Martin Luther King, Jr. Day, Valentine's Day, Easter, the Fourth of July, Thanksgiving, and Christmas. Other ideas revolve around sports events (such as the Super Bowl), Black History Month, the school-year schedule, and ecclesiastical seasons such as Advent and Lent.

Use these ideas to celebrate annual occasions and establish traditions in which the group can share. When a group has a common experience, its members grow closer, caring and supporting one another. By simply participating in annual traditions and customs, the youth will make memories and grow closer to one another.

NEW YEAR'S EVE PARTY

Kick off the New Year with an overnight party full of fun and memories. This event, like other overnights, means staying up all night and eating junk food, with one exception: At midnight, start the year off with a special service. One option is to have Communion at the stroke of midnight; invite the pastor to be part of this service. (The youth will be amazed the senior pastor is awake at midnight!) Other worship ideas include meditation; singing praise and worship songs; or holding a prayer, foot-washing, or covenant service where the youth pray about, discuss, and determine the expectations of the group for the coming year. Any other activity that helps the group begin the year focused on God works too.

A New Year's Eve party wouldn't be complete without New Year's resolutions. Have each student write his or her resolutions on a piece of paper then seal it in a self-addressed envelope. In addition to typical resolutions, give the kids a chance to make spiritual resolutions. You might provide a questionnaire that asks the youth to complete partial sentences such as these:

- In relation to my faith, I resolve to …
- One thing I'm going to change this year is …
- I want God to help me with …
- I will improve relations with my family by …

Add partial sentences as you see fit. Save the envelopes until the following year, and mail them right before Christmas so that the youth receive them between Christmas and New Year's. This memoir gives the youth a measuring tool to see how they did on their resolutions, and a point to consider for their resolutions for the next year. If you do not wish to wait a whole year, mail the envelopes in July so that they help the youth refocus on their resolutions.

For another fun option on New Year's Eve, create a time capsule. This device is a weather-proof container filled with everyday items and information about the current time. The container is then buried—literally or figuratively—for a set number of years determined by your group. The capsule is not opened until that date. One suggestion for an opening date is eighteen years from the time you bury it: the graduation year of the current year's newborns. Or have the opening date coincide with the senior class's twenty-year reunion, since many students will be in town for their high school reunions. I recommend a minimum of ten years; young people's perceptions change a lot over that amount of time, but the world doesn't change that much.

Ask the youth to bring small items for the time capsule such as CD inserts, newspaper articles, and photos. Include a price list of common items such as a gallon of milk or gasoline. Have each kid write a personal message to be opened in the future. (Warning: Be careful when including technology in your time capsule, because today's high-tech equipment could go the way of the eight-track player and five-inch floppy.)

VALENTINE DINNER

Valentine's Day is a day for spending time with that special someone and letting him or her know you care. From the time we were little kids in grade school, we made valentines to hand out to classmates and ate chalky candy hearts. Somewhere along the line, Valentine's Day was supposed to change into something more serious between two people. But not everyone has a special someone with whom to share this holiday. So have a youth group Valentine's dinner for everyone, including couples and individuals, to celebrate and have fun.

Ask parents or other volunteers to host a dinner for the youth. The main focus should be celebrating those we hold dear, such as friends, family, significant others, and Christian sisters and brothers. Keep this dinner from being a couples-only, romantic event, or else some youth won't participate.

Decorate a room at the church, and serve a nice meal with music playing in the background. Have pens and heart-shaped paper and available for youth to write Valentines to one another. As the youth leave the event, hand out small, heart-shaped boxes of candy with a valentine from God reminding the kids that they are loved.

To create a twist on this event, have the youth host a dinner for the entire church. Offer tables for two for couples looking for a more private dinner, and larger tables for groups that want to engage in more fellowship during dinner. Singles—young and old—will appreciate the ability to sit with one another, as will couples seated with other couples.

Showcase the teens' musical talents by having live background music during dinner. For ambience, put tablecloths, place mats, candles, and centerpieces on each table. You might also dim the lights and plug in those white Christmas lights to create an outdoor, under-the-stars feeling. (This event can serve as a fundraiser too.)

SUPER BOWL PARTY

Kick off America's favorite unofficial holiday with a memorable bash filled good food, good friends, good commercials, and (if you're lucky) good football. Usually played the last Sunday in January, the Super Bowl is the biggest sporting event of the year. This hype makes for an easy-to-organize youth group party.

Watch the game in the church youth room or at someone's house. Have the youth bring snacks to share, and order pizza or giant sub sandwiches.

Hold a contest to guess the half-time and final scores. Also, have the kids rate the commercials, which people often find the most entertaining aspect of the Super Bowl. The youth can give awards for the funniest, most imaginative, most ridiculous, most boring, most memorable, and so forth. NFL or Super Bowl trivia contests also provide fun.

While football interests some youth, let's face it: Others don't know the difference between a first down and a touchdown. For this reason, provide a second TV or other activity for non-football watchers.

If your group prefers another sport, have the party during the World Series, NBA Finals, Daytona 500, or whatever event your group fancies.

BLACK HISTORY MONTH CELEBRATION

February is Black History Month, a perfect opportunity to celebrate African American history and culture. Many youth today are comfortable with people of different ethnicities, but that situation hasn't always taken place. Throughout America's history, certain groups of people have been discriminated against because of race. One prominent example is the African American struggle for freedom and equality. In some regions, this struggle still continues. Although we should be aware year-round of African American contributions to our country, culture, and faith, use February to focus on them.

Here are some ideas for making this month memorable for your teens:

- Highlight famous African American "heroes of the faith" each week in church or youth group. (For names of heroes, check out *Young Lions*, Abingdon Press, 2001; ISBN 0-687-09937-4.)

- Learn and sing African American spirituals in worship. Delve deeper, discovering the hardship and hope in the stories that inspired these songs. Try to sing them as they were intended to be sung (without a harpsichord or twelve-string orchestra). Check your church hymnal or songbook for good songs.

- Invite guest speakers to youth group. You probably don't need to look far to find such people; they might be members of your church. Former members of the Tuskegee Airmen, those who played baseball in the Negro League, and people from other historically significant groups make excellent speakers.

For an outing, take your group to a museum that features exhibits celebrating African American art, music, or history.

MARCH ON [YOUR TOWN NAME]

On August 28, 1963, Martin Luther King, Jr. led the March on Washington, advocating equal rights for all US citizens. Dr. King's deliverance of his "I Have a Dream" speech from the steps of the Lincoln Memorial has become one of the most famous events in modern times. To celebrate Dr. King's life and message, organize a March on [your town name]. This event will give the youth an opportunity to learn more about the civil rights struggle in the 1950s and 1960s and about Dr. King.

Schedule your march on Martin Luther King, Jr. Day or the weekend before that day. To make an impact on the entire church, arrange with your pastor make the youth group's march the main message of the worship service. For a dramatic presentation, have the youth process as a group to the front of the sanctuary during the service, singing songs and carrying banners and signs. (To get ideas for signs and banners, enter *March on Washington* into your browser to find thousands of websites on the march.) This presentation is most effective if only the pastor and youth know it will happen and surprise the congregation.

After the youth march down the aisle, let the congregation hear the "I Have a Dream" speech. You might assign different parts to each youth to read aloud, or you might show the video of Dr. King speaking. Following the speech, have the youth discuss their feelings about Dr. King's words. To conclude the service, ask the congregation to join hands and sing "We Shall Overcome" or another appropriate song.

If this idea won't work during your church's worship time, schedule your march for immediately after the service or some time during Martin Luther King, Jr. Day weekend. Publicize that your youth group is honoring Dr. King at a community rally at a specific time and a place such as your church, the steps of city hall, or another central location. The rally should include music, readings, and a time for remembrance. Instead of reading just from the "I Have a Dream" speech, read excerpts from Dr. King's many letters and speeches.

In the presentation, include members of your congregation who lived through this volatile time in our country. Perhaps your church has members who saw Dr. King speak, participated in a sit-in or boycott, or even attended the March on Washington. If so, ask them to discuss their experiences. (These same people are a great resource for youth group lessons and discussions during Black History Month.)

EASTER CELEBRATION

On the Saturday before Easter, have the youth group host an Easter celebration for the children in the church and in the community. The celebration should include games, egg coloring, egg hunts, and a short Easter devotion message.

Your group can conduct simple games such as duck-duck-goose and an "egg" toss using water balloons. Activities can include pony rides, puzzles, and a reading corner with stories. Art projects can include egg decorating, as well as making bunny puppets out of paper bags, construction paper, and markers.

When it comes to egg hunts, organize separate hunts for different age groups. (There are fewer ways to ruin your celebration than when a fourth grader knocks over the three year olds while racing to find as much candy as possible.) Save the egg hunt for the end, because once children have candy they tend to tune out and it's hard to get them to focus on anything else.

For the devotion, have the youth tell the Easter story to the children. The teens can relay the story by reading the Bible, using their own words, acting it out, or using a puppet show. Encourage the children to have fun with Easter but to remember that the real focus is on Jesus, not candy. Close in prayer, and let the children continue with the celebration.

EASTER SUNRISE SERVICE

I know it's early, but it's also one of the best services of the year. So have the youth group lead the Easter sunrise service. Some people would consider having to get up for the sunrise a punishment, not a blessing. But they'll soon realize that the true blessing comes from greeting the day with praise to God. And what better way to celebrate Jesus' resurrection than to proclaim the good news first thing in the morning?

Let the youth plan and lead the morning worship service. An outdoor setting contributes to the unique atmosphere. Bad weather can pose a challenge; but when it cooperates, this service is spectacular. Worshiping under the dome of the sky above, without the closed roof of a building, makes one feel closer to God. Remembering the morning Jesus was raised from the dead at a celebration in the morning will give the youth a another perspective on the Easter story. The music is unique to that time of year, the prayers are more personal, and the message seems more real when delivered outside in the morning air.

Easter sunrise service also provides an appropriate time to baptize youth and others from your church. In the early church, new Christians were baptized only at Easter. Each year, many people look forward to this wonderful and ancient tradition.

To make the service even more memorable, hold it at a unique outdoor location. A local park, beach, mountain, hilltop, forest, or cemetery will add a new dimension to your service. A graveyard may seem kind of creepy at first. But when you consider that the Easter story takes place in a graveyard and you're celebrating Jesus' resurrection from the tomb, you might find that a graveyard is the perfect place for a sunrise service.

YEARBOOK-SIGNING PARTY

Do you remember the excitement of getting your yearbook, flipping through each page to see how many times you were pictured, and looking up your friends to see what they had to say? Yearbooks are fun for everyone and hold memories that last a lifetime.

Yearbooks also seem to have an adverse effect on students' ability to focus on what's happening in youth group. It seems the more yearbooks in the room the harder it is for students to pay attention. They open and flip through yearbooks as if they're drawn by the gravitational pull of a black hole located in the pages. Well, here's an idea that lets kids spend all of the time they want looking at yearbooks and saves you from getting frustrated by kids not paying attention: a yearbook-signing party.

Designate one youth group meeting as a yearbook-signing party where the youth can bring yearbooks for their friends to sign. If you have youth from different schools in your group, this party gives those kids a chance to see and sign one another's annuals. Spend the meeting perusing the yearbooks' pages and listening to stories from the youth as they discuss memories from the past year.

If you have a youth group yearbook, hand out copies at this party. This way, everyone will have something to sign and to be signed.

SCHOOL'S-OUT PARTY

End the year and kick off your summer schedule by having a school's-out party. This event should include games, food, and a celebration of the end of early mornings and homework for a while.

Pull out your craziest games, have bags of chips and other snacks, and encourage the youth to bring friends. This party is the culmination of months of hard work, so the youth can blow off steam and rid themselves of the tension and stress built up during final exams.

To create a truly memorable event, make the party a lock-in or lock-out. Lock-ins involve youth staying in the church all night, and lock-outs involve the group staying out all night. The latter requires more energy and planning, but youth love the thought of being up all night and out having fun.

You'll need to plan some safe activities for lock-outs, since the parents probably won't like the thought of their kids roaming the streets all night. See if a movie theater offers midnight showings, or check out midnight bowling at a local alley. Another late-night option is broomball at an ice rink. If any of these activities take place twenty-four hours a day, you can do any combination of them.

You'll also need food for the lock-out. So how do you find a restaurant open at 3:00 A.M. that youth will like? Some fast food places have drive-thru windows open twenty-four hours a day. But ordering at a drive-thru for more than a few people gets confusing; plus, you probably don't want the youth eating in the church van. So contact the manager or owner of the restaurant and arrange for the lobby to be opened just for your group. The youth will feel special when the doors are open just for them and they have the whole place to themselves.

Finish up your lock-out with breakfast at another restaurant, or ask the parents to cook breakfast back at the church. By morning, the youth will be tired and ready to sleep. Before the teens go home, give them a calendar of summer activities or a reminder about the next youth group event.

A school's-out party is a fun way to wrap up the school year, renew friendships, and kick off your summer youth group schedule. This annual celebration will quickly become an eagerly anticipated event.

INDEPENDENCE DAY BARBEQUE AND FIREWORKS

Are you looking for a memorable way to celebrate Independence Day with your group? How about a barbeque and fireworks? The Fourth of July is one of the best days of the year to have an old-fashioned barbeque with traditional elements such as hot dogs, hamburgers, potato salad, chips, and watermelon. A potluck works well for this event.

In addition to food, have outdoor games for the youth, such as soccer, capture the flag, and kick the can. (Don't forget the watermelon-seed-spitting contest.) Give prizes for farthest distance, shortest distance, most stylish, messiest, and best multiple-seed shot. Provide a football, softball, bat, and Frisbee® for youth who want to play catch.

Host the barbeque at a local park or at the home of one of the youth. Parks have open space for field games and activities, but you'll need to call ahead to reserve your spot, because the Fourth of July is a popular day at parks.

If you can, arrange to have your celebration at a place with a pool, lake, or river nearby. If the celebration takes place at a teen's home, hook up a sprinkler to run through and tape together giant sheets of plastic to slide on when they become wet. Swimming and water activities are a favorite for youth, and the water will provide a refreshing reprieve from the heat. If any of the families have boats,

ask them to take the kids water skiing and tubing or just for a cruise on the water. If you rent a houseboat, you could have the barbeque on the water.

As the day winds down and the evening begins, move the group to a location with a fireworks display. The ideal situation is to have the barbeque at a park where a fireworks display will take place. If fireworks are not visible from a local park, have the group relocate for the highlight of the evening.

Designating this celebration as a family event makes it better. The parents will appreciate getting together, the younger siblings will appreciate being "cool" like the teenagers if they win the watermelon-seed-spitting contest, and the youth will have fun talking about how embarrassing their parents are. For a fun activity, you might have a parents-versus-youth family softball game.

Schedule a time for a devotion, where your group discusses what it means to live in a nation where we can freely worship God. Explain that we shouldn't take that freedom for granted and that we should always pray for persons in other countries who are persecuted for their belief in God.

YOUTH GROUP POOL PARTY

Since teenagers love pools, have a youth group pool party. If a family in the church has a pool big enough for your group, ask the family members if you could have the party at their house. If your group is too big for a residential pool, rent the pool of a local school, park, or recreation center.

For the party, have the youth invite friends and meet at the pool for a fun time of splashing, diving, and cannonballs. This event doesn't require much structure on your part—the youth will have fun just swimming and hanging out with their friends. You can have a contest for the biggest splash from the diving board or for who can hold his or her breath the longest. Just don't over-structure your time at the pool. Give the teens the chance to organize games of Marco Polo and Sharks and Minnows on their own.

Adding food to any youth event makes it better, as long as the youth like the food. Order pizza, giant subs, or other party food, and the youth will enjoy the event more. You might combine your party with a barbeque.

If your group doesn't have a pool nearby, drive to a pool. The youth will appreciate and remember the rare occasion when they went to a swimming pool. An indoor pool during winter works well too.

BACK-TO-SCHOOL PARTY

Most youth don't want to celebrate going back to school because they would rather not attend school. But this time of year is the perfect opportunity to kick off the youth group program for the school year. Teens have more energy and interest in participating at the beginning of the year before they get overly committed to school activities and worn out by studies.

Host a huge back-to-school party, and ask the youth to invite friends to join in the festivities. Include games and activities you normally don't have. If your budget allows, rent inflatable games such as sumo suits, a Velcro® wall, moon bounce, or obstacle course. You'll hear plenty of laughs during these fun games, and the youth will relay stories after the party. Play games that make newcomers feel welcome, and get the youth to interact with people they don't know very well.

You can also hold this party as a lock-in where youth spend the entire night "locked in" the church. Have midnight snacks, and let the kids stay up late. Your back-to-school party will help you get a jump on the school year and get the youth involved right away.

STEP-UP SUNDAY

Does your church or youth group do something special for step-up or advancement Sunday (the Sunday when everyone moves up a grade and joins a new class)? This day is most significant for kids moving into their first year of youth group.

To make incoming youth feel welcome, plan a special party where they are the guests of honor. Send out personalized correspondences inviting each potential new member to the party. Explain to each newcomer that lots of new people will attend and that he or she won't be alone. Before the party, tell your group these new kids must feel welcomed, accepted, and a part of the group so that they will come back. One affirming gesture your group can offer is to explode in cheering and applause whenever a new person is introduced. The recipients will find this response overwhelming but uplifting.

As part of the celebration, recognize each grade level and those advancing to the next grade. Begin with the graduates, and work down to the newcomers. At each grade level, ask those in that grade whether they have any words of wisdom to pass on to those stepping up.

For another idea on celebrating step-up or advancement Sunday, see Hail and Farewell: Passing the Torch on page 55.

SEE YOU AT THE POLE

See You at the Pole (SYATP) is a national movement of students who meet to pray around the flagpole at their schools. Held every year on the third Wednesday of September, SYATP is a chance for students to join in praying for the school year ahead. The teens pray for teachers, students, administrators, the whole school, and the community supporting their school. Students meet on campus and form circles around the flagpole, offering prayers aloud and silently for a designated time. Some SYATP meetings include singing and invitations to Christian student organizations and clubs.

Organized and led by students at local schools, SYATP is open to all who want to join in the prayers. SYATP aims to unite Christians in praying on the same day (the third Wednesday in September), at the same time (7:00 A.M. local), and at a common location at school (flagpole) all across the country.

For more information about See You at the Pole, Challenge Sunday (the Sunday before SYATP), or ideas for adult volunteers, visit www.syatp.com.

HAUNTED HAYRIDE

It's a dark night, and your youth group is on a hayride out in the country when something goes wrong and the tractor pulling the trailer sputters, jerks, and dies. Now you're out in the woods or the middle of a field and it's pitch black. As the driver of the tractor tries to figure out what's going on, the sudden and unexpected rattling of a chain saw pierces the night, shattering the silence. Screams fill the air as the youth search in vain for the origin of the frightening sound. They can't find the chain saw because a parent hidden from sight is at the controls. As a matter of fact, there's nothing wrong with the tractor and your kids are safe—but do they know that fact? These elements are all part of a haunted hayride.

This event requires a lot of coordination and planning among volunteers. First, find a place to have a hayride. Second, enlist parents who are willing to be out in the cold to startle youth. Then find a chain saw without the chain. (Don't worry; it's the unmistakable sound of the chain saw engine that's more terrifying than anything else.) And finally, you'll need a group of youth willing to have fun and thrills on a hayride. Determine whether to tell them it's haunted.

Once you have the place, volunteers, and supplies, assign a driver to the tractor and design a course that allows various scary elements to occur during the ride. Then arrange to have the parents hidden along the course and ready to spring into action when the tractor and trailer pass by. Jumping out, shooting silly-string, banging metal trash can lids together,

and dropping plastic spiders out of a tree will frighten the youth. You might dress someone up as a scarecrow and perch him or her on a stick or in a chair along the path. Or better yet, place the scarecrow on the trailer before the youth get on, and when they get close, watch them jump when the scarecrow comes to life. Make sure the setting is dark, and keep flashlight use to a minimum.

Youth enjoy this activity even without the haunted part. So if a hunted hayride doesn't work for your group, just take a regular hayride—it's a ton of fun. Another option is to go to a corn maze, which is literally a maze in the corn. Your kids will like playing this game in the daytime and will like it even more in the dark. Make sure each youth has a partner and a whistle so that no one gets lost.

All of these options will make memories for your group. To wrap up the evening, have a campfire and make S'Mores. While the kids are eating, have a short devotion about God's protection and how we're held in the palm of God's hand.

TRUNK-OR-TREAT

This alternative to traditional trick-or-treating offers fun for children at your church and community. The youth group provides a safe place for children to trick-or-treat where parents don't have to worry about the candy being handed out or the people their children are around.

Shopping malls often have a trick-or-treat night where kids in costume go from store to store collecting candy. Doing so is safer than roaming the streets, and children can cover lots of ground in a short time and relatively short distance. These same elements make trunk-or-treat appealing to both children and parents.

Youth and other church members park their cars nose-in or parallel to the curb along the edge of the parking lot, creating an enclosed area for children to trunk-or-treat. The participants pop open the trunks of their cars, place candy in the trunks, and wait for the children to make the rounds. The parents and children walk from car to car, showing off their costumes and receiving treats. Let the youth truck-or-treat after all of the kids have had a chance to get candy. This way, the junior high and senior high youth can get their candy fix without going door to door or getting into trouble.

Encourage the youth and the adults to dress in costume too. You could have a theme and get everyone to come in a costume that fits the theme. If your church is hosting a fall festival or other Halloween alternative, add truck-or-treating to the activities to get the youth involved.

TURKEY-BOWL FLAG FOOTBALL GAME

What says Thanksgiving more than football? Well, turkey for one, and family for another, and pilgrims for another, thankfulness too—OK, so a lot of things say Thanksgiving more than football. But for many, the holiday isn't Thanksgiving without football. So start a tradition by having an annual youth flag football game, and dub it the "Turkey Bowl." Play the game the Sunday before Thanksgiving.

The day of the game, divide the group into two teams and let them have fun playing flag football (the type of football in which the advancement of the ball is stopped by removing a flag attached to the ball carrier's clothes). For the flag, provide a rag or brightly colored cloth. If you want to have a trophy for the winning team, spray paint a small football gold and have the team's members sign it. If you don't want to keep score, just have everyone sign the ball. Then put the ball in the youth room for display.

Tell the youth to be prepared for rain, mud, and cold—the muddier, the more fun the game will be. Divide up the teams so that both have even number of boys and girls, athletes and non-athletes, junior high and senior high, and so forth. Encourage the older members of your youth group to include younger kids by giving them chances to run and catch the ball. To make the game even fairer, have a parent or other adult be the quarterback for both teams. %

After the game, take photos of the group, warm up with hot cocoa, and laugh about the Turkey Bowl.

YOUTH-LED CHILDREN'S ADVENT CELEBRATION

Advent is a season of preparation for the coming Christ child. While the world is focused on Christmastime consumerism, your youth can use a children's Advent celebration to reinfor and remember the real meaning of the season. Have the celebration the first week of Advent or the weekend after Thanksgiving. Begin the season with a time when children learn about, and make small reminders of their learnings to take home and use during the season.

Include a wide range of activities from games to arts and crafts. Have the youth teach the children about chrismons and then make them together. Chrismons are Christian symbols used for decorating Christmas trees. As chrismons are made, have the youth explain the symbolism behind each design. See if the children can come up with their own chrismon designs.

Advent wreaths are another fun symbol to make. Have each person make his or her own miniature wreath to use throughout Advent. As the kids are making the wreaths, have the youth talk about what each candle represents (first week: hope, second week: peace, third week: joy, fourth week: love, and the Christ candle in the center).

After making their unique decorations, you might participate in decorating the church for Christmas. Often combined with a churchwide hanging-of-the-greens, this event gives people a chance to paint the windows, drape garlands, put up lights, and set up trees in the church. Use the chrismons the kids made to decorate the church.

Wrap up the celebration with a reading, reenactment, puppet show, or skit of the Christmas story in Luke 1-2:21 and Matthew 1:18-2:12 to remind the youth of the true focus of Christmas.

LONGEST-NIGHT SERVICE

For most of us, the holiday season is a time of celebration. But for some, the holidays bring sadness because of losses in their lives. Bad childhood experiences, the loss of a job, financial hardships, and the death of a loved one are a few reasons the holidays are not be a joyous time for all.

One of the hardest times is the longest night of the year, the winter solstice, which occurs around December 20, the day with the least amount of sunlight. Being alone for any amount of time is difficult when you are used to having someone by your side. But this day is especially hard for those grieving a loss.

Hold a special service the night of winter solstice to help those who are hurting. Offer this service to the whole church or to just your teens. If your group has lost a member, this service can help. Bringing people together in times of pain lends support and encouragement to the entire group. Some people might have difficulty attending this service, but it is a vital way to help those who are struggling. It also provides a way for youth to deal with the circumstances together, an essential element of grieving.

CHRISTMAS PARTY

Celebrate Christmas with a youth group Christmas party. Gift exchanges often take place at a youth group Christmas party, and you can do them several ways. Your group can choose a theme, have a spending limit, give serious, white-elephant, or gag gifts, choose Secret Santa partners, draw numbers, or have a grab-a-gift exchange.

Your group has several options for the destination of the Christmas party. You might host it at the church, in the youth room, or at a group member's house. Some groups combine a progressive dinner where gifts are exchanged after dessert at the last stop. Other groups go Christmas caroling before exchanging presents. Some groups do service projects as their Christmas party; for example, some visit a nursing home to share the party with those who might feel lonely at Christmas.

For a service-oriented gift exchange, try a nothing-in-return exchange. Ask the youth to bring gifts to be given to others, with no expectation of receiving a gift in return. Then take these gifts to those in need. You might donate the items to a homeless shelter, or drive around and deliver them to the homeless in parks and on the streets.

Any way you choose to conduct the party, wrap it up with a devotion about the true gift of Christmas: Jesus Christ.

LESSONS AND CAROLS

Are you looking for a memorable way to involve the youth choir in your church's Christmas celebration? Try a Lessons and Carols or Hymn Sing service, a tradition that involves the whole church. Lessons and Carols is a service introduced to the Anglican Church by E. W. Benson, later Archbishop of Canterbury, and was first performed in on Christmas Eve in 1880 in Great Britain. The traditional services consist of nine carols and nine lessons. Have the youth choir lead this traditional service of worship and celebration in which music and Scripture tell the Christmas story.

If you wish, customize your Lessons and Carols service to include both modern Christmas songs and traditional favorites. The youth choir should sing some pieces by themselves but should also include songs and carols for the congregation to sing along with. Lessons and Carols is intended to be an act of worship, not a concert or performance. Congregation members will be touched by this musical and Scriptural telling of the birth of our Savior, and Lessons and Carols will quickly become a highly anticipated holiday tradition.

If a less formal hymn-sing fits better with your church, the choir may sing only traditional Christmas carols and hymns. These pieces are the

annual favorites most people are used to hearing and singing around Christmastime. All of these carols are based on Scripture passages, and with a little planning you can arrange the songs into an order that matches Scripture. Between songs, read a Scripture that leads into the next set of songs.

Make the hymn-sing a family event and decorate the sanctuary (or wherever you're holding the service) to look like a family room in a house. A mock fireplace, rocking chair, and couch give a cozy feel to any room. Invite children to come, sit on the floor, and hear stories read by a youth sitting in the rocking chair.

However you choose to use music and Scripture, to celebrate Christmas, both the youth and the congregation members will remember the event as a favorite.

YOUTH GROUP REUNION

Instead of saying goodbye to graduating seniors and pushing them out the door never to see them again, have a youth group reunion. Plan the reunion around a holiday when you know students will be back home from college. The week between Christmas and New Years usually works well.

Send invitations to former youth while they are at school. Also publicize the event around the church so that former youth who didn't leave home know about the reunion.

For the reunion, plan some time for former youth to discuss with current youth what they've been up to since graduating. Take photos and celebrate everyone being together, as people do any reunion.

The youth will enjoy this fun annual tradition, because they'll get to see older members of the group whom they haven't seen in a while. Former students enjoy this event because they get to see friends they haven't seen since leaving for college. And the entire group will enjoy reliving the good memories and funny stories from past years.

CHAPTER 7
MILESTONES

I remember the day I got my driver's license like it was yesterday. I went to the DMV after school, skipping cross country practice. I backed over only one cone before getting that magic piece of paper. I felt so grown up and ready to face the world. I also remember the fear and anxiety I felt on my first day of high school, worried that I'd be tormented by seniors.

Milestones are memories in themselves, because they occur only once in someone's life. This chapter is different from the others in that you don't have to create the memory. For example, you can't make someone turn thirteen or get

straight A's. This chapter provides ideas for marking those milestones and celebrating along with youth when they reach them.

Milestones, like markers along the road measuring the distance one has traveled, signal the progress youth have made in their journeys toward adulthood. Reaching a milestone is the apex of one part of the longer journey, and youth live for those moments. So read on and discover some ideas to help you celebrate those special times. From starting junior high to graduating high school, this chapter has ideas for adding a special touch to those moments in life.

MILESTONES

STARTING HIGH SCHOOL

The transition from junior high to high school marks a significant milestone. Celebrate this special occasion with a youth group celebration for those starting high school. As part of the celebration, ask the new high schoolers to discuss what they're excited or nervous about, and have the older youth relay words of wisdom and other tips for surviving high school.

Send a handwritten card, note, or letter to all of the students entering high school, congratulating them on reaching this milestone. Let them know you are excited for them as they make this next step. In the correspondence, invite them to a welcome celebration where they are the guests of honor.

To make this transition easier for the newcomers, assign mentors to them. Pair the new high schoolers each with a senior high student who check in with them to see how they're doing. This mentoring will make adjusting to high school a bit easier and less intimidating for younger members of your group. Plus, freshmen and sophomores feel important when they have an upperclassman for a friend.

Make this milestone a memorable one by helping new high school students feel welcomed, prepared, and supported. The beginning of high school is when most youth fear being dumped in a garbage can or getting a swirly, since these stories are passed down from year to year. So have your group be supportive and affirming during this transition.

BECOMING A TEENAGER

Becoming a teenager is an important milestone in a young person's life. Turning thirteen marks the transition from a little kid or pre-teen to an official teenager. Even if turning thirteen isn't celebrated in America the same way it is in other places around the world, your youth group should celebrate those having this birthday.

Giving special recognition to those celebrating their thirteenth birthday will lift up and recognize teenagers as special individuals who are loved by God. If you have a large group with many kids turning thirteen around the same time, have one party for all of them. If your group is smaller and you know in advance that someone is turning thirteen, plan a surprise party.

Involve your whole youth group in the celebration by asking the older youth to organize a party or special celebration during a youth group meeting. Have the older students make and sign a giant card for the special birthday honoree, ask them to bring cupcakes for everyone, or let the youth determine the best way to celebrate.

In addition to the group celebration, have your adult volunteers send personal congratulations and celebratory notes to the new teens. You should also write a letter to the thirteen year olds telling them how special they are to you and to God and that you look forward to watching them grow and mature in their faith as part of the youth group. Telling the new teens you're happy they've reached this milestone lets them know that you care and that they are loved.

Becoming a teenager is the first of the important age milestones (such as sixteen, eighteen, and twenty-one) youth reach, and in their lives it's the most significant to date. Acknowledging and recognizing this milestone will add to the special memories carried throughout students' lives.

EIGHTEENTH BIRTHDAY

What's the only thing better than becoming a teenager or turning sixteen and getting your driver's license? Becoming an official adult!

Most youth find turning eighteen exciting because, now they can excuse themselves from school and sign permission slips without their parents. Many restrictions are removed at this age, and many eighteen year olds think now they don't need their parents as much. (Little do they know what lurks around the corner.)

Celebrate eighteenth birthdays as a group, acknowledging that these youth are arriving one step closer to full adulthood by reaching this milestone. Have the entire group sign a giant homemade birthday card to be given to the person turning eighteen. Check out the affirmations on pages 60–62 for more ideas for celebrating.

As the youth worker, write a letter to the youth when they turn eighteen, congratulating them on their birthday and letting them know that you are proud of the growth you've seen in them. Take a few lines to explain what is different after reaching this milestone. Legally speaking, at age eighteen youth become adults; they are held to a higher level of accountability, and the consequences they can face are much greater than what they've been used to. Let the youth know in your letters that you're willing to walk with them through anything they face in this time of transition. Reaffirm that you care for them and that they are valuable to the group, the church, and the world.

Turning eighteen and becoming an adult is an important step in a young person's life. The youth will remember the celebration of this momentous occasion for years to come.

STARTING JUNIOR HIGH SCHOOL

One of the first significant signs that a child is growing up happens when they leave elementary school for junior high school or middle school. This transition is exciting for youth because they are leaving the "child" behind and moving up the ladder one rung. It's scary because they are entering the unknown that comes with leaving what is familiar (although youth will rarely admit this fact). These changes, along with the physical changes to their bodies, create an enormous amount of insecurity, which manifests itself in a youth's desire to belong to a group.

To make this transition less intimidating and more inviting, welcome new youth into the group with a celebration befitting royalty. OK, maybe you don't have to go that far, but make it special. Have the existing members of the group host a welcome party for those stepping up and entering youth group. (See Step-up Sunday on page 82.) As part of the celebration, have current junior high youth give tips for surviving junior high school. Spread lots of attention and caring over the newcomers, making them feel important, valuable, and welcome. It's easy to get them to come to a special event, but it's more important to get them coming back week after week and investing themselves into the youth ministry.

Before you throw the party, send a card, note, or letter to all students entering junior high or middle school, congratulating them on reaching this milestone. Let them know that you're excited to get to know them better and that they are welcome at youth group and in your office anytime. In this letter, invite them to the welcome celebration where they are the guests of honor.

Get a good start with new youth group members. Beginning junior high or middle school marks a significant milestone for youth, and celebrating this accomplishment by spoiling newcomers with an enthusiastic welcome and acceptance is a great way to begin their time in youth group.

GETTING A DRIVER'S LICENSE

Turning sixteen usually means one thing: getting a driver's license. This milestone is perhaps the biggest, because youth gain more freedom and responsibility when they can drive on their own. For their entire lives, youth have known driving as something adults do, and now that they can drive they are one step closer to being an adult.

For most youth, turning sixteen isn't about being older; it's about being able to drive. So celebrate with your students who reach this age and get their driver's licenses. Keeping a record on the wall of the youth room with how many times each group member had to retake the test before he or she got a license probably isn't the best way to affirm youth. Instead, mark this milestone with a celebration and special recognition at your next youth group meeting. Some groups present new drivers with a key chain or other small gift such as a tire-pressure gauge, ice scraper, bottle of car-washing soap, mini-flashlight for the glove compartment, sponge and bucket, or a five-dollar gift card to help with that first tank of gas.

If you are willing, start a youth group roadside-assistance program. Youth receive a membership card with emergency phone numbers to call if they need help. Enlist a parent or two who would be willing to receive calls at any hour of the night to help youth when they have a dead battery, flat tire, or other emergency need. Or have a day of workshops where youth learn basic automotive survival skills such as changing a tire and jump-starting a car.

Whatever special help with driving you decide to offer students who receive their driver's licenses, send each of them a letter of congratulations. Include a few words on the awesome responsibility that comes with driving and how others' lives are in the hands of the youth every time they're behind the wheel. Let them know that nothing is so important that it's worth taking a life or damaging a vehicle. And if you are brave enough, include in the letter an invitation to take the youth out for an ice cream or burger—the student drives, you pay.

With the growing trend of graduated driver's licenses in many states, you might need to adapt this idea to fit your group. Getting a driver's license is huge for youth. Congratulate, celebrate, and affirm your youth when they reach this milestone. And give them a good fifteen-minute head start before you leave youth group to drive home!

GRADUATION DINNER

For many youth, graduation is the crowning accomplishment of their brief but filled life. They have been working toward this goal since they were five years old. Since the majority of their lives have been focused on education, graduating from high school is the zenith of milestones.

One way to celebrate this achievement is by offering a special gift to the graduating youth. Many churches give devotion books or bookmarks to graduating seniors.

In addition to a book, give them the gift of a nice dinner with their fellow youth group members. The dinner can be a homemade meal at someone's house, or it can take place at a fancy restaurant. Choose a place that works best with your budget and your group.

If your group takes interest in a local event, use it to go along with your senior dinner. For example, if your group loves pro sports, take the group to a baseball game and have hot dogs and soda while watching the local team. No matter what you do, take photos and give each youth a copy for his or her personal scrapbook. (See page 52 for Video Yearbooks.) By spending time to mark this milestone with your graduates, you can celebrate and congratulate them on their accomplishments.

During the dinner, ask each senior to discuss his or her plans for after high school. Whether the youth plan to go to work, college, the military, or simply do not know their plans, the seniors will have an idea of what one another will be doing when they relay this information. Ask the graduates to tell favorite stories from their time in youth group, and then relay your thoughts on their time in the group. Your graduates will remember this dinner for a long time, and it may just be the last time all of the seniors are During Christmas break, invite all of the graduates to a youth group reunion. (See page 86.)

SENIOR SUNDAY

For a churchwide celebration of high school graduation, have a Senior Sunday. Choose one Sunday around graduation time to highlight the accomplishments of your graduates. Reserve seats in the front of the sanctuary, so that the graduates may sit there with their families. During the service, recognize the graduates and have them come forward for a special blessing. After the service, hold a reception where church members can meet and talk to the graduates.

If you're looking for a more interactive way of marking this milestone, involve the graduates in the service. Have them usher, pray, read Scripture, play music, and preach.

Some churches have a tradition where graduates process in at the beginning of worship, wearing their caps and gowns. The graduates all sit together during the service then recess out of the service at the end. This tradition allows the whole church to see all of the graduates at once, including the mix of school colors represented in the caps, robes, and gowns that youth wear.

BACCALAUREATE

Baccalaureate is a religious service celebrating the completion of non-graduate-level studies. The word baccalaureate means a farewell sermon delivered to a graduating class. Once a main part of graduation festivities on campus, the baccalaureate tradition has in recent days become more scarce. Often held in a local church, a baccalaureate marks the milestone of graduation.

Plan a service that gives thanks to God and celebrates the accomplishments of the graduating youth. Have prayers for continued guidance of the students starting a new chapter of their lives, since these prayers are an important part of baccalaureate.

If you wish, work together with youth workers in your community to organize an ecumenical service. Rotating the site of baccalaureate will keep it a community event that is not dominated by one church.

Wherever you hold the baccalaureate involve the youth in the service. Invite them to read, lead prayers, conduct music, sing solos, usher, and deliver the message. For a twist, invite one of the teachers or staff from the school to be the guest speaker at baccalaureate.

BAPTISM AND CONFIRMATION

Two of the greatest milestones in a person's faith journey are baptism and confirmation (also called reaffirmation of baptism). Mark these special moments in a youth's life by celebrating his or her commitment to God.

Churches have their members baptized in various ways: sprinkled, poured, or immersed. Some youth were baptized as infants and have no memory of their baptisms; other youth remember their baptisms because they were elementary-age children when they decided to be baptized.

Most churches and denominations offer confirmation for youth when they are in junior high or middle school. Being confirmed involves study, prayer, and learning what membership of one's church means. All of these aspects lead to a point where the youth confirm their beliefs, claim their faith, and join the Christian and local denominational church. At confirmation, youth reaffirm their baptism and join in the covenant their parents made when they were infants. If a youth wasn't baptized as an infant or child, he or she may be baptized before confirmation.

If you have students who wish to be baptized, make the setting special by choosing a different location, time of day, or date. But remember that baptisms in the name of God the Creator, Jesus Christ, and the Holy Spirit are valid and equal. So celebrate all baptisms without holding one above another.

When you celebrate a student's baptism or confirmation, have the older youth tell stories of their baptisms or confirmations and discuss the difference these events have made in their lives. Send affirming notes, cards, or letters from the group to those being baptized or confirmed. You might present these letters to the participants as part of the service. Or you could have the youth group videotape the service and give a copy to each confirmand or newly baptized student as a gift. However you want to mark this occasion, include the entire youth group.

Confirmation and baptism are important milestones in a person's faith journey. So make sure your youth know how special they are and how much they are loved.

COLLEGE STUDENT REUNION SUNDAY

Former youth love to return to the church and fill everyone in on how their life is going at college. They are excited to see the familiar faces of people they know care about them and receive affirmations from the church family they grew up with. So have your church sponsor a College Student Reunion Sunday. During this Sunday, college students who are home for break can be recognized and lead worship. Planning this event takes a little organization, since the former youth may be spread out all over the country, but thanks to e-mail this regrouping isn't as difficult as it used to be.

Pick a theme, and assign roles to different college students. If you find assigning roles in advance too complicated, arrange to have simple ways to plug in college students the day of the service. Ask everyone to arrive early so that you can go over the service together. After the service, hold a reception so that congregation members have an opportunity to interact with the college students.

If your church allows, have the college students wear sweatshirts from their schools. It's fun for the congregation to see what different schools are represented, and the students will have fun showing their school pride. This option will prove especially entertaining if there are rivalries among schools.

If you're looking for an activity outside worship service to get college students together, check out Youth Group Reunion on page 86. Whatever type of activity you choose for a reunion, include college-age young adults who didn't go to college but were members of your youth group.

MAKING A TEAM OR OTHER ORGANIZATION

Most youth participate in some sort of extracurricular activity. They have various levels of ability in many areas, and we must recognize each student's accomplishments no matter what his or her ability or involvement. Some youth might be starters on a team, play first chair in the orchestra, serve as president of a club, or have the leading role in a school play. Other youth from your group sit on the bench, play eighth chair, or help out as stagehands and never appear on stage. All of these accomplishments are equally important and are milestones to the students.

Mark these accomplishments with special recognition, using anything from certificates of congratulations to a wall or bulletin board of accomplishments and photos. This affirmation acknowledges the achievement and hard work each student has put into the activity.

All of the examples given above are extracurricular activities in a school, but don't forget about civic organizations, community involvement, recreational sports, Special

Olympics, volunteer programs, job promotions, service organizations, and scholastic achievements such as honor roll and perfect attendance. (Your local newspaper might print the names of students achieving these honors, so check the newspaper for your students' names.)

After you hear of an accomplishment, send a note or card congratulating the teen on his or her involvement. Let the students know in these notes that you'd like to attend events involving their activities. (See Come-See-Me Cards on page 43.) If you can, volunteer to help in their organizations.

Recognizing and celebrating the milestone achievements in young people's lives is vital. Doing so gives the teens the support and encouragement to follow their dreams and continue to develop their skills and talents.

BECOMING A CHRISTIAN

The decision to accept Jesus Christ as Lord and Savior may be difficult for some and easy for others. When a youth does make the decision to enter into a personal relationship with God, acknowledge this significant milestone.

With the student's permission, let the youth group know his or her decision. The church exists to provide support and community for one another because living as a Christian is impossible to do alone. Therefore, the youth group should embody the supportive community that God calls us to be. When a member of the youth group makes a first-time commitment to Christ, the entire group should celebrate and give thanks. The Christian should be recognized so that the group can pray for the person as he or she starts this new journey.

Your group might also choose to present a gift to a person when he or she makes such a commitment. Great gifts include a Bible and a book of prayers and letters written by other members of the youth group. If you give the latter to the teen, include a page from the pastor of the church.

Celebrating a person reaching the milestone of deciding to commit his or her life to Christ is important and essential. But their journey with Christ doesn't end there. So work as a group to continue supporting one another in your walks together. You may want to form prayer partners or accountability partners within your group. Because we all have faults and lose focus at times in our lives, we need to be surrounded by Christian friends who will not judge but offer support.

When a youth who has lost focus realizes he or she is not centered on God and makes a rededication, celebrate. Like the prodigal's father (Luke 15:11-32), openly welcome the student and throw a party. (Don't you think God is celebrating that a child has returned?) Present a small gift to the youth who rededicate their lives to Christ as a reminder that they are never alone and that they are loved unconditionally. The gift can be a card, photo, charm, or certificate. As a group, have a special way of marking and celebrating the youth who rededicate their lives to Christ.

CHAPTER 8
FUNDRAISERS

Fundraising probably doesn't enter your mind when you think about good memory makers, but it can be a fun experience that youth remember. When I was a youth, we would go door to door selling candy to raise money for school and church trips. We also had annual rummage sales, talent shows, and car washes. The youth group at my wife's childhood church has hosted an annual Easter pancake breakfast for a long time. (Some church members are convinced that Jesus himself stopped by the church for a plate of pancakes as nourishment for his walk on the road to Emmaus).

But sometimes it's not enough to just have a pancake breakfast or a car wash. Nowadays you have to be creative and come up with fundraising projects that both youth and the congregation or community will enjoy and support. This chapter includes these kinds of ideas. And not only will church members find the fundraisers enjoyable, but your youth will have a blast doing them.

Take a pie in the face, plant two dozen plastic flamingos in a yard, let church members in on a special ISO (Initial Stock Offering) opportunity, or pick up something for yourself at a youth auction. Use these ideas and the others in this chapter to raise money for youth group trips, camps, missions, tours, and other outreach or service projects, and have fun while you're at it.

FUNDRAISERS

FLOCKS OF FLAMINGOS

WARNING: *This fundraiser assumes that having plastic, pink flamingos in your yard would be tacky and unwanted. Some people will not see the deterrent, and some will be downright offended that you don't consider pink flamingos appropriate yard décor.*

For a set amount of money, members of the congregation can send a flock of flamingos to other people. Take orders, and tell people that birds will be delivered during a designated time, such as during July or over the next week. This fundraiser requires your group to acquire at least twenty of the pink, plastic, foul fowl.

When delivering flamingos, some groups wait until after sunset then plant them in yards at night when recipients are unaware. To make this fundraiser more exciting for youth, pretend you're on a covert mission and it's important that you not get caught. Photograph or videotape the deliveries to show at youth group. Whether you deliver the flamingos at night or during the day, it's important that you have several youth to help so that the yard decorating is done quickly. After a set period of time (such as twenty-four hours, three days, or one week), collect the flock and move it to the next recipients.

A large group of pink birds in the front yard of a house will get lots of attention from neighbors and others who pass by. Make a sign that explains why the flamingos are there, and plant it with the birds. The sign should contain a simple message such as, "Youth Group Mission Trip Fundraiser." Be careful not to damage lawns.

Another way of conducting a Flocks of Flamingos fundraiser is to deliver only one bird to each yard and ask the recipients to bring the flamingos back to church the following Sunday. Or let each recipient enjoy more of the fun by passing the bird on to the next recipient. For this option, attach a list of people who are in line to receive the bird so that the recipients know whom to pass it on to.

Any way you do it, the flamingo fundraiser provides fun for your group and the church. People will talk about those plastic, pink lawn ornaments for years. The best part of this fundraiser is that no one will have to clean up droppings!

NOTE: *You may have difficulty finding these pink flamingos during the winter months. Supercenters, local nurseries, and online stores are probably the best places to find flamingos. Collect all of your pink flamingos before planning or advertising this fundraiser.*

GNOME-INAL FUNDS

This activity is exactly like Flocks of Flamingos but with garden gnomes. Browse through garage sales or the garden section of your local home or hardware store to find the tackiest gnomes possible.

FLAMINGO INSURANCE

If certain members of your church feel that the Flocks of Flamingos fundraiser is for the birds, offer flamingo insurance. For a certain amount, congregation members can purchase insurance that protects their yards from an invasion of pink, plastic flamingos. To get the most sign-ups for flamingo insurance, wait to offer it until the Flock of Flamingos fundraiser has been receiving orders for a couple of weeks.

Increase insurance sales by publicizing some of the names of the flamingo recipients-to-be. Don't publish all of the names, though. You want people who aren't on the list (or aren't on the list yet) to also purchase flamingo insurance. Adding a removal fee for when youth come collect flamingos might also encourage people to buy the insurance.

For a twist, have the insurance cover only a certain number of flamingo purchases. For example, the insurance would cover three purchases per recipient, but if four or five people pay to have flamingos delivered to the same household, then the insurance is used up and flamingos get delivered. However, a person could purchase more than one policy.

The best part of this fundraiser is that you'll make money without much overhead cost. If you're lucky, someone in your church will like or collect pink flamingos and will offer to buy them from the youth group after the fundraiser is over. Congregation members will appreciate the creativity and will probably enjoy purchasing flamingos for their friends as much as the annual youth spaghetti dinner.

COINS IN A JAR

Here's a "cents-able" way to raise money: The youth group collects change in glass jars with different people labeled on each jar. The person whose jar gets the most money receives a special prize such as a whipped-cream pie in the face, a bucket of slime dumped on his or her head, or an hour in the dunk tank at the churchwide picnic.

For this contest, recruit easy targets to be competitors, such as senior pastors, youth leaders, youth, or parents. The more popular and well-known the participants, the greater the success your fundraiser will have. This event works well over the course of a few weeks.

Place each competitor's photo on a glass jar, then set the jars where church members can access them. Congregation members can place coins and bills in the jar of the person they want to see win the prize. For some reason, youth directors frequently win this competition.

Each week, announce the total of each jar and encourage people to continue giving their spare change. After a set number of weeks, add up all of the money and declare a winner. Have the winning prize presented at a special ceremony

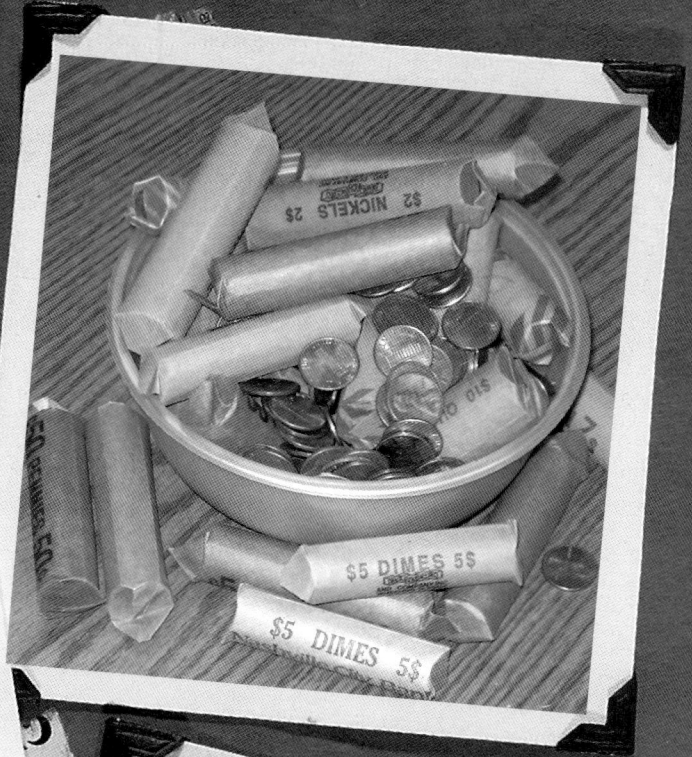

after church or youth group. If a churchwide event such as a variety show has been planned, award the prize at that time.

To make more money, assign different values to each coin or bill. For example, all coins are face value, except quarters, which are double their face value. You can even make it so that paper money counts against the total. So if a jar has $72 in coins and $50 in paper money, the jar's total is $22.

To help bring in more money, award a prize to the winning participant for every twenty-five dollars in his or her jar. If the winning jar has fifty dollars in it, then its respective participant gets two pies in the face or two buckets of slime dumped on him or her. To add a few more dollars to the fundraiser, auction off the privilege of throwing pies or dumping buckets.

Coins in a Jar is an entertaining, visual way to raise money. People have fun competing, and most people like to see someone get slimed or dunked.

VENDING BOOTH AT THE FAIR

For a fun and memorable fundraiser, have the youth group run a booth at a fair. If your group has a gift for crafts, make items to sell at a booth. Or maybe a food booth would suit your group. Selling food at a fair requires lots of work and planning, but the rewards are worth it. This fundraiser, if done well, can raise so much money that you don't have to do any other fundraisers for the year.

If a vending booth isn't suitable to your group, try directing and parking cars in the lots around the fairgrounds. If your church is close to the fairgrounds, offer parking in the church lot. Or check into helping with garbage cleanup; it's not the most glamorous job, but it will help your youth group raise money.

If you decide on a parking service, offer a car wash for an extra fee. Festival attendees can get a car wash while enjoying a day at the fair. To

provide efficient service, have a parking team and a car-washing team operating at the same time.

For information on vending booths, parking lot attendants, and other opportunities at the fair, contact your local county or state fair offices. For other festivals and events in your community, contact your local chamber of commerce.

BUY A MILE

Are you going on a mission trip, choir tour, or other youth trip and looking for an easy way to raise money without doing a lot of work? Make a large map of your trip, and clearly mark the route your group will travel. Figure out the total number of miles and the amount it will cost your group to travel those miles. Include rental car or bus fees, gas, food, lodging, and any incidentals. Divide that total amount by the number of miles your group will travel; the quotient is your cost per mile. Encourage congregation members to help the youth reach their destination by buying miles. Sell five or ten miles at a time.

You can also "sell" gallons of gas. Figure the gas mileage of the vehicle you'll drive and how many gallons the trip will require. Use the current cost of gas to sell gallons in an attempt to fill the tank.

This fundraiser can help cover building supplies for a mission trip. If you are building a house, offer church members the chance to buy a brick, window, door, or two-by-four stud. If you're doing home repairs such as painting or roofing, let people buy a can of paint, bag of cement, shingles, and so on. Instead of a map, make a poster depicting a house and with a writing utensil fill in the bricks, windows, and so forth as the church members purchase them. This option works especially well if your group is going on a local mission trip that doesn't require a lot of driving but does require money for supplies.

This fundraiser is a fun way to involve the church and raise the money you need for your trip. The visual aid of a poster helps communicate to the church how much money has been raised and how much is still needed. And it helps educate church members about the coming youth group trip or project. If you do build a house or take on another construction project, take photos so that when you return you can show people what they've purchased.

TAKE STOCK IN . . .

Raise money for a mission trip, retreat, camp, or other youth project by having church members take stock in the coming event or project. In this fundraiser, the youth sell shares of stock for a certain amount of money. People can buy as many shares as they want. Each shareholder receives a postcard from a youth on the trip, a ticket to a post-trip slide show and dessert, and a personal report from one of the participants.

First, decide how many stocks you need to sell by simply dividing the total amount you want to raise by the amount of each stock. Then advertise the amount of stocks available for purchase to let people know the shares have a limited availability. Ask the youth who are going on the trip or participating in the project to help sell the stock. Have them explain to buyers why they're going on the trip and what the group will be doing.

Print up stock certificates with the name of the event, a certificate number, the stockholder's name, and the number of shares purchased. Have one of the youth sign the stock certificate.

If you wish, each share of stock could buy a specific item. For example, a ten-dollar share of stock could buy one piece of lumber for the big playground toy the youth will be building on their summer mission trip to an inner-city housing development. Don't worry about being exact with the numbers; you're just giving people a clear idea of what their stock will buy.

This fundraiser doesn't require a lot of work, but make sure you follow through on sending postcards, producing the slide show, and having the youth deliver personal reports.

SPORTING EVENT

Many college and professional sports arenas have opportunities for groups to raise money. Some allow non-profit groups to work in the vending booths or help with cleanup. And wouldn't your youth group have fun selling hot dogs, pretzels, nachos, popcorn, and candy at a local sports arena? Youth love this fundraiser because they get to go to a big event, and since the work keeps them busy the time goes by fast. If your congregation is tired of fundraisers, selling food at a sporting event might be a good option.

Cleaning up after an event also helps raise funds. After a sporting event or concert, arenas and stadiums contain lots of litter. Sweeping aisles, clearing stairways, and picking up trash after the big game will be appreciated and will help your group raise money.

Contact your local arenas and stadiums to see if your group can get involved. And remember that opportunities such as baseball, football, hockey, basketball, concerts, conventions, and rallies come up year round.

Depending on the venue, you'll need lots of youth and adult help, including parents and older adults. Make sure that the event is appropriate for the youth to hear or see while they're serving food or waiting for the event to end to help with cleanup.

DINNER AUCTION

Dinner auctions are popular, because people get something for themselves while giving to a cause. For your youth group's auction, have the teens solicit donations of items from local businesses, members of the church, or any other source. Encourage the youth to be creative; you'll want a wide variety of items, ranging from babysitting service to restaurant gift certificates. Make sure each youth donates something to the auction, whether it's his or her time (piano lessons, yard work, e-mail lessons, and car detailing) or objects he or she has made (such as craft projects and homemade jam).

On the day of the auction, set the items on tables. Choose some items to be in a silent auction, and save ten to fifteen big money makers, such as a fishing trip with the pastor or a dinner for ten by a church member who is a chef, for the live auction. People have fun competing against one another in live auctions, which often raise more money than silent auctions.

As people arrive, give each person a written set of rules, including the silent auction closing time. Give each guest a bid number written in large numbers on a piece of cardstock, and log who has which number. The guests will write their bid numbers on the bid sheets at the silent auction and hold up their cards to bid at the live auction. These numbers work well if many people attend or if you don't know all of the attendees. You don't want the auctioneer to be embarrassed because he or she doesn't know the names of the bidders raising their hands.

In a silent auction, individuals write their bids (by writing either their names or their bid numbers) on a sheet of paper in front of the item. At the end of a set period of time, the bid sheets are collected and the highest bid wins that item. Before the auction, print the bid sheets with the name of the item, description of the item, any limits or expiration dates, and approximate retail value. Choose a starting bid (twenty-five to fifty percent of the value works well). Then determine the bid increments (such as fifty cents, a dollar, five dollars) and clearly write the increments on the bid sheet so that people don't increase the bids by small amounts such as one penny. Provide plenty of pencils at the silent auction tables. When the bidding closes at the predetermined time, quickly close the bidding by having the volunteers either highlight or circle the winner and collect all of the pencils. Watch out: People sometimes become competitive at the close of a silent auction!

Live auctions are conducted aloud, with people bidding on items presented by the auctioneer. Have fun with the bidding. If one item is called "Three-Youth Yard Service for Three Hours," have the three youth come up on stage, show off their muscles, and roleplay how much yard work will get done in three hours. Ask a couple of volunteers to help as spotters to identify bidders who are raising their bid cards. Have the live auction items available for people to view ahead of time, or write descriptions in the program so that people have a chance to read about what will be sold in the live auction.

To cover the cost of the dinner, ask for food donations or charge money. That way, you make sure that all of your auction proceeds are profit.

Auctions are a lot of work; but if they are done well, they can bring in a lot of money. Like most fundraising events, auctions require organization and advertising for several weeks in advance. They also involve youth, parents, and the congregation in a fun and memorable activity.

BONUS CHAPTER

What's Inside

- Calendar layout ideas, pages 104–105
- Witness statement handout, page 106
- Parent Bible study flier, page 107
- Senior banquet and recognition handout designs, pages 108-109
- Come-see-me card example, page 110
- You-were-great card example, page 111
- Have-a-great-week card example, page 111
- Scrapbook page layout idea with journal entry, page 112

Calendar-newsletters are easy ways to create a sense of group identity and excitement about your group. Recruit several of your tech-savvy youth to create the designs for the calendar-newsletter. Include a "good gossip" column, so that they get to read about the positive things that are going on in everyone's lives.

JULY

Crosswalk Student Ministry

Our Mission: To Creatively Engage Students So They Become Passionate Followers Of Jesus Christ!

SUN	MON	TUE	WED	THU	FRI	SAT
		1	2	3	4	5
6	7	8	9	10	11	12

The CSM Office will be closed July 3–4, 6–11, and 23–27.

YOUTH PLUNGE 2005 Info Meeting

JULY 1, 7:00 pm
Fellowship Hall

All students who are going and their parents should attend.

All money and permission slips must be turned in.

No Room Changes Will Be Made After Noon on July 2.

First Church
123 American Way
Anytown, USA 54321

CSM Office Phone
333-222-1111

Emergency Cell
333-223-3251

CSM DIRECTOR
David Jones
David@firstchurch.org

• 10,000 Youth
• Worship
• Learning
• Service
• Games
• Fun

Bands
10:00–2:00

SEE ATTACHED FLYER FOR MORE DETAILS!

13

Summer Celebration
All MS and HS Students
6:00–8:30 pm
Look for the tents behind the church!

14

3V Bible Study

Younger HS
July 14
6:00–7:30
Room 204

Older HS
July 15
6:00–7:30
Room 204

Living life God's way

15

16

Rising 9th Grade Girls Bead Party Space is limited. Call Courtney for more info!

Rising 9th Grade Guys Movie Night. Call Drew for more info!

17

Rising 6th Grade Girls Bead Party Space is limited. Call Mandie for more info!

Rising 6th Grade Guys Putt Putt Night. Call Drew for more info!

18

19

CSM

20

Summer Celebration
All MS and HS Students
6:00–8:30 pm
Look for the tents behind the church!

21

3V Bible Study

Younger HS
July 21
6:00–7:30
Room 204

Older HS
July 22
6:00–7:30
Room 204

Living life God's way

22

YOUTH PLUNGE 2005
July 23–27

Cool Speakers!
Awesome Bands!
Florida Beach!

Contact David or Mandie for more info.

BE THERE!

27

Summer Celebration
All MS and HS Students
6:00–8:30 pm
Look for the tents behind the church!

28

3V Bible Study

Younger HS
July 28
6:00–7:30
Room 204

Older HS
July 29
6:00–7:30
Room 204

Living life God's way

29

30

31

Synago Small Group Leaders Meeting
July 31, 5:00–7:00

SUMMER THEME: WILD, WILD WEST

We will have the mechanical bull and several great games during Summer Celebration. Our band, The Youthies, will lead worship. Invite all your friends! See you there!

Courtney Smith
UGA Junior
(Rising 9th Grade Girls)
Homecourt@gadogs.com

Drew "Red" Green
Mercer Sophomore
(Rising 9th Grade Guys)
Redgreen@bearmail.com

Mandie Monroe
Tennessee Grad School
(Rising 6th Graders/MS)
Govols@bigomail.com

CROSS WALK STUDENT MINISTRY

Leading the Way to Christ

Did You Know?

As of June 22, 200 students and 148 parents of students have joined First Church since August 1999!

WITNESS STATEMENT HANDOUT

Creating a clear and understandable witness statement will help you communicate your faith to non-believers. Sometimes we're caught off guard when people ask us about our faith, so if we think about what we will say ahead of time we will be much more prepared and successful.

COMPLETE THESE SENTENCES TO HELP YOU FORM YOUR WITNESS STATEMENT:

1. I RECEIVED CHRIST WHEN . . .

2. MY EARLY EXPERIENCE AS A CHRISTIAN WAS . . .

3. Christ has changed my life by . . .

4. I still struggle with . . .

5. the Bible verses that help me the most are . . .

When you answer questions about your faith,

do
- pray for guidance
- be authentic
- refer to one or two Bible verses that illustrate your point

don't
- get preachy or dramatic
- be too wordy or beat around the bush
- be too general

COMMON GROUND PARENT-AND-YOUTH BIBLE STUDY

Beginning the first week of summer, come and learn how to not only survive the parent-teen relationship but also to thrive as you grow together as a family.

Sessions include

- raising teens,
- raising parents,
- the world through the eyes of a teenager,
- liking each other,
- conflict resolution, and
- putting God at the center of the parent-teen relationship

Generating publicity helps create a sense of unity and makes lasting memories for youth groups. When you build up your studies and events with advertisements, such as the flier above, not only will your group remember to attend but they will also keep these events in their memories. (See page 32 for planning ideas on parent-and-youth Bible studies.)

SENIOR
RECOGNITION
May 18, 2005

CROSS WALK
STUDENT MINISTRY

Leading the Way to Christ

CROSSWALK STUDENT
MINISTRY

First Church
123 American Way
Anytown, USA 54321

Phone: 555-122-4321
E-mail: David@firstchurch.org

SENIOR
RECOGNITION

Peachtree City Church

CROSS WALK
STUDENT MINISTRY

Leading the Way to Christ

May 18, 2005

ACTIVITIES

- Seniors recognized in worship—11:00am.
- A special bulletin with pictures of seniors to be distributed.
- Banquet for all students, parents, family and friends to honor seniors—6:00 to 9:00pm.
- Senior Leadership Award, Senior Music Award, Senior Service Award presentations.
- Year In Review Video debut.

CROSSWALK STUDENT MINISTRY

For your seniors, make a big deal out of graduation. They will never forget how special they felt because the church supported them and sent them on to greater things. Above is an example of a bulletin with information about a senior banquet. To recognize the seniors and let church members know about the dinner, mail or hand these bulletins out at your church. See page 91 for more details on planning the dinner.

YOU ARE INVITED
TO JOIN US
IN THIS CELEBRATION!

May 18, 2005

Please RSVP

Call

David Jones

555-122-4321

CROSSWALK STUDENT MINISTRY

Seniors will be recognized at the
11:00am
worship service.

CROSS WALK
STUDENT MINISTRY

Leading the Way to Christ

A banquet will be held from
6:00 to 9:00pm
in Bryan Fellowship Hall.

Cost is $10 per person.
Seniors eat free!
RSVP

FIRST CHURCH

Here are an example of a come-see-me card (referred to on page 43) and affirmation cards. Having these cards available facilitates opportunities to make lasting memories with your youth.

Come See Me

Event name: _____

Where: _____

When: _____

Cost: _____

Ice cream afterward? Yes ____   No____

You Were Great!

Thanks for inviting me to

_____. You did a great job, and I loved watching you in your element. I think it's great how you live your faith in everything you do. You are special to me and to God!

In Christ,
[Your name]

Have a Great Week

Just a note to say, "Have a great week and I'm praying for you." Remember that God will never leave you. Trust in that! You are special to God and to me. See you Sunday!

In Christ,
[Your name]

Put your pictures and memories into books. As with the example below, have at least one youth from each picture write about what was going on when the picture was taken.

I would call this picture "Divin' In," because when we got out of the church van, we just ran and jumped off the dock and into the water. I've had some awesome memories in youth group before, but this one will for sure be at the top of the list.

Everything was perfect that day. When we sat around the campfire for dinner, I just knew that God was there—even when we were just hanging out and having fun. I think that's the first time I ever noticed that we don't have to be in church or singing praise songs for God to be with us. God was there on that beach, just hanging out with us. It was awesome!

—Molly Smith